100 WALKS IN
Hereford & Worcester

compiled by

V·AN GREAVES

The Crowood Press

First published in 1994 by
The Crowood Press Ltd
Ramsbury
Marlborough
Wiltshire SN8 2HR

British Library Cataloguing-in-Publication Data
A catalogue record for this book is
available from the British Library

ISBN 1 85223 785 6

All maps by Janet Powell

Typeset by Carreg Limited, Ross-on-Wye, Herefordshire

Printed in Great Britain by Redwood Books, Trowbridge, Wiltshire

CONTENTS

73. Queenswood Country Park and Westhope Hill 7m (11km)
74. A Fownhope Circuit 7m (11km)
75. Stoke Prior and Marston Stannett 7m (11km)
76. Overbury and Bredon Hill 7m (11km)
77. ...and longer version 9m ($14^1/_2$km)
78. Alvechurch and Rowney Green 7m (11km)
79. Fromes Hill and Bosbury $7^1/_2$m (12km)
80. Knightwick and Martley $7^1/_2$m (12km)
81. Richards Castle and High Vinnals $7^1/_2$m (12km)
82. Old Storridge Common & Alfrick $7^1/_2$m (12km)
83. Kingsford Country Park $7^1/_2$m (12km)
84. Wigmore and Lingen 8m (13km)
85. Mamble, Menithwood and Lindridge 8m (13km)
86. Goodrich and Coppet Hill $8^1/_2$ m ($13^1/_2$km)
87. Kington and Rushock Hill $8^1/_2$m ($13^1/_2$km)
88. Ross-on-Wye and Penyard Park $8^1/_2$m ($13^1/_2$km)
89. Bromyard and the Frome Valley $8^1/_2$m ($13^1/_2$km)
90. Abberley Hill and Woodbury Hill $8^1/_2$m ($13^1/_2$km)
91. Whitbourne $8^1/_2$m ($13^1/_2$km)
92. ...and longer version 11m ($17^1/_2$km)
93. Mordiford 9m ($14^1/_2$km)
94. Leintwardine and Downton Gorge 9m ($14^1/_2$km)
95. King's Thorn and Hoarwithy 9m ($14^1/_2$km)
96. Wyre Forest (Route 2) 9m ($14^1/_2$km)
97. Ewyas Harold and Abbey Dore 9m ($14^1/_2$km)
98. Hay Bluff and Black Hill $9^1/_2$m (15km)
99. ...and longer version $10^1/_2$m (17km)
100. Weobley, Dilwyn and Kings Pyon 10m (16km)

PUBLISHER'S NOTE

We very much hope that you enjoy the routes presented in this book, which has been compiled with the aim of allowing you to explore the area in the best possible way – on foot.

We strongly recommend that you take the relevant map for the area, and for this reason we list the appropriate Ordnance Survey maps for each route. Whilst the details and descriptions given for each walk were accurate at time of writing, the countryside is constantly changing, and a map will be essential if, for any reason, you are unable to follow the given route. It is good practice to carry a map and use it so that you are always aware of your exact location.

We cannot be held responsible if some of the details in the route descriptions are found to be inaccurate, but should be grateful if walkers would advise us of any major alterations. Please note that whenever you are walking in the countryside you are on somebody else's land, and we must stress that you should *always* keep to established rights of way, and *never* cross fences, hedges or other boundaries unless there is a clear crossing point.

Remember the country code:

Enjoy the country and respect its life and work
Guard against all risk of fire
Fasten all gates
Keep dogs under close control
Keep to public footpaths across all farmland
Use gates and stiles to cross field boundaries
Leave all livestock, machinery and crops alone
Take your litter home
Help to keep all water clean
Protect wildlife, plants and trees
Make no unnecessary noise

The walks are listed by length – from approximately 1 to 12 miles – but the amount of time taken will depend on the fitness of the walkers and the time spent exploring any points of interest along the way. Nearly all the walks are circular and most offer recommendations for refreshments.

Good walking.

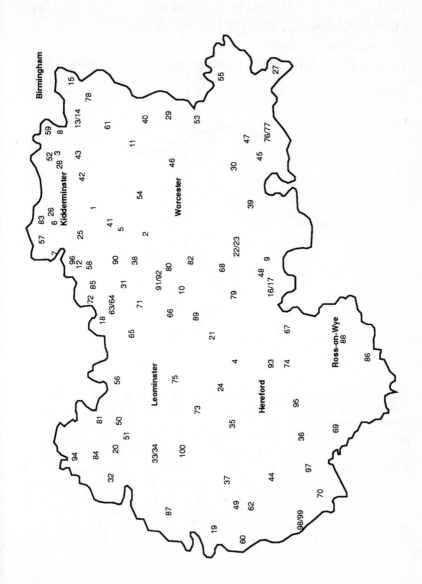

Walk 1   **HARTLEBURY COMMON**   2m (3km)

Maps: OS Sheets Landranger 138; Pathfinder 953.

A walk for nature lovers.

Start: At 826715, the parking area on the Common off the B4193.

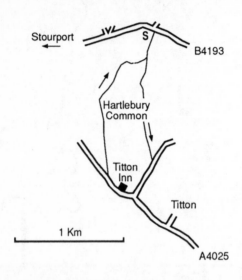

One can walk almost anywhere on numerous paths within the 216 acres of this fine Common. The suggested route from the car parking area goes past the covered information board to reach a broad sandy track. This heads, through gorse and grasses, towards electricity pylons and is waymarked by blue arrowed posts. Just before the edge of a fir plantation, take the left fork when the track splits. Go through fennel bushes to reach a clump of oak trees on the left. Here, the track forks again: take the right-hand track, which, in effect, heads straight on in the same direction. Go over at a sandy cross-roads and then gradually descend to where the track starts to bend to the right. Here, look for a blue arrowed post and a track going sharply left. Take this track to an oak wood where another track is joined. Turn right. At the first entrance on the left, note Titton Mill, a fine building, set back from the track. Pass a hard-core track on the right, staying with the lane to reach the A4025. Turn right and follow the main road, with care, to reach the **Titton Inn**, where refreshments are possible.

Continue from the inn to reach a point opposite an off-licence. There is a sign to an industrial estate just beyond and opposite this (on the side you are walking), you should go back on to **Hartlebury Common** again. Go under twin sets of electricity pylons, keeping roughly parallel to the ridge on the right. Any one of two or three tracks will do here. Now look for the edge of a modern housing estate on the left, through the shrubs and trees. When you are level with this, pick up a track which goes right into a shallow valley decked with Turkey Oaks. The track now climbs and bends left. Keep left at a junction: there are occasional views out over Stourport and the Abberley Hills from this rim. Keep left at another junction and meander round to where the path opens out on to a sandy patch. Here a lateral broad path is met: simply turn right and in about 200 or more yards, return to the car park.

POINTS OF INTEREST:

Titton Inn - The pub, and area surrounding it, derives its name from the phrase 'the tit on the Inn' referring to the well-known common bird.

Hartlebury Common - Long regarded as one of the most important heathlands in the West Midlands, Hartlebury Common supports a whole range of wild plants, animals and birds. It is a Site of Special Scientific Interest, managed by Hereford and Worcester Countryside Service. It consists of mainly dry, lowland dwarf shrub heath situated on a river terrace, (formed by the adjacent River Severn). Topsoils are very sandy and, in fact, can, where not colonised by plants, be shifted by the wind, thus forming an almost unique inland sand-dune environment. This sand lies on top of Triassic sandstone rock layers. The area is good for butterflies, the rare Green Hairstreak butterfly occasionally being seen here.

REFRESHMENTS:

The Titton Inn, on the route.

For a range of alternatives, Stourport is only about 1 mile away.

Walk 2   MONKWOOD NATURE RESERVE   2m (3km)

Maps: OS Sheets Landranger 150; Pathfinder 974.

A naturalist's delight.

Start: At 804606, the car park on the lane splitting the Reserve.

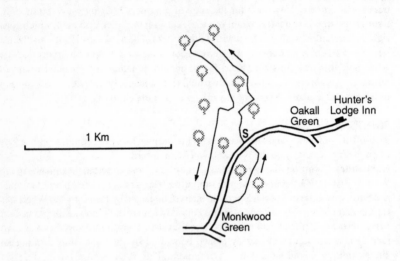

Note that except for the public footpath and bridleway, all other paths in the **Reserve** may be closed at short notice. They are always closed on the 1st February to prevent public rights of way becoming established.

   The walk takes a figure of eight shape, so could be completed as a pair of short outings.

   From the car park-cum-picnic area, turn left and go through the gate with the blue arrow to reach a marked bridleway. Where the woods clear slightly there is a splitting of ways: keep right, and before the next blue arrow you will reach a path going off to the right. Take this, following it through thinned out woods and then bearing left by some silver birches, where there are two options. Take the right-hand path. This path, possibly muddy, follows the edge of the wood, with a field seen through the trees to the right. Eventually, after a patch of thick woodland, a tiny arrowed post points left. (Just right of this arrow there is a boggy pond).

Follow the new path to reach a T-junction. Turn left and continue to reach the bridleway again. Turn left and walk more comfortably for several hundred yards to reach a small clearing. There, turn sharp right, noting the nesting boxes on a prominent tree. Now, take the first major track on the left. Some distance along this there is track on the left which reaches an area of marshland apparently developed to encourage wetland species. Regain the track, noting a property set back in the trees to the right, and continue to reach a lane, crossing directly into the other portion of woodland. Bear left by the first green arrow on a post. Ignore the next post/green arrow and pass a bench to find another post/green arrow pointing straight on. Follow this to arrive at a T-junction. Turn left on to a green track leading back to a gate, a lane and, opposite, the starting car park (which has a public footpath sign to Ockeridge Wood).

POINTS OF INTEREST:
Reserve - The, albeit small, area of woodland that is Monkwood Nature Reserve is a Site of Special Scientific Interest, part of the Worcestershire Nature Conservation Trust and the British Butterfly Conservation Society. It is a 154 acre reserve, opened in June 1987 by the well known artist Gordon Benningfield. Monkwood is a very ancient woodland which has probably existed since the last Ice Age, 8,000 years ago. It has a wealth of wildlife, some species being rare. In early June, the walker will probably spot the fragile Wood White butterfly, a species confined to certain British woods. In August or September, a more difficult insect to spot is the Brown Hairstreak butterfly, a much more rapid flyer. Further information on the Reserve is available from the Worcestershire Nature Conservation Trust, Hanbury Road, Droitwich, Worcestershire WR9 7DU (tel: Droitwich 773031) or the British Butterfly Conservation Society, 47 Stagborough Way, Blickhill, Stourport on Severn DY13 8SY (tel: Stourport 4860).

REFRESHMENTS:
The nearest available spot is *The Hunter's Lodge*, Oakall Green.

Walk 3   A CLENT HILLS INNER CIRCUIT $2\frac{1}{2}$m (4km)

Maps: OS Sheets Landranger 139; Pathfinder 933 and 953.

A short, picturesque walk over two hills.

Start: At 938807, Nimmings Visitor Centre car park.

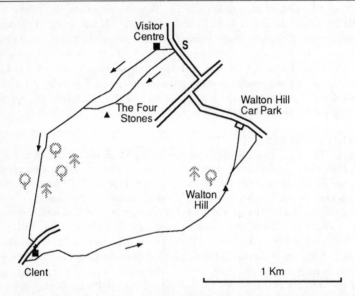

Begin by either going out of the car park and doubling back to climb via twisted beech roots beneath stately trunks, or go on to the obvious path, graded for those who are disabled. The former path climbs a crest lined with beech trees, and with fine views to the left to Walton Hill, to emerge on to an open, undulating broad ridge. Continue to reach the **Four Stones**, a trig. point and, just left, a toposcope. The latter path winds gently along the side of the hill, with shelter and benches, to reach another panoramic toposcope. One can double back to the summit and Four Stones from here.

From the top a broad path descends to a clump of sycamores. About 100 yards beyond these, two benches straddle the path, some yards apart. Aim for the left-hand one and go down towards some firs ahead, with a shallow valley on the left cradling more firs. Enter the trees, the pleasant path passing both deciduous and conifers. Ignore a post with an arrow, to the left, keeping straight on as the path opens out with glimpses of the deep valley between the hills, to the left. Follow a wire fence, to the left, then go either side of an old bench and descend steeply, bearing round to the left to zig-zag down to a post with two blue arrows. Take a U-turn here to join another path coming in from below near a blue arrowed post. Now follow iron railings to come out by some cottages and take a metalled drive to reach a lane. Turn right, and then left by the church of St Leonard. Immediately past the lych gate, turn left into an alley which borders the churchyard to reach a stile. Cross and go up a field, with ever increasing views of the valley and hills. Go over a stump in a hedge and a further field to reach a stile at the edge of woods. Go over to join a path coming in from the right and walk past the National Trust sign for Clent Hills.

The broad path climbs steeply with a hedge and field to the right and Turkey Oak trees to the left. The view is excellent and it is worth pausing at the bench dedicated to Hilda and Ron Smith to rest and admire. Now gradually ascend to the summit of Walton Hill, at 1035 feet (315 metres). About 100 yards beyond the top, bear left on to a track which descends the hillside to reach Walton Hill car park. Turn left along the lane and, at the bottom, go right by a green. Now take the next left to return to the Nimmings car park and Visitor Centre.

POINTS OF INTEREST:
Four Stones - These stones are not at all ancient, they were erected by the Lyttleton family of Hagley Hall.

The views are excellent from several points on the walk.

REFRESHMENTS:
Available at the Visitor Centre, when it is open.

Walk 4   **Shucknall Hill and Westhide**   3m (5km)

Maps: OS Sheets Landranger 149; Pathfinder 1017.

An interesting short walk with plenty of variety.

Start: At 587427, in Shucknall at a space about 100 yards off the main A4103.

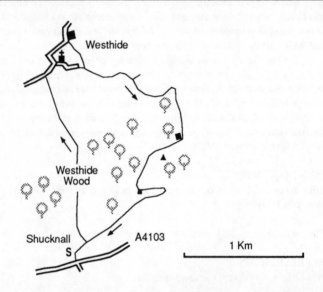

From the off-road space, two ways present themselves. Turn to the right and take the longer looking lane gently uphill. Pass 'The Paddock', a property to the right, to reach, just beyond, a green track going uphill on the left. This reaches some cross-ways: go straight ahead, aiming for a thatched cottage. Go alongside this and pass an underground reservoir, to the left, by twisting around a gate and entering a wood. A good track is now followed to a cross-roads. Go over and descend through a small pocket of rhododendrons. Note an arrow on a fir tree and cross another track. On the far side of is a footpath, by a board, leading uphill. Follow this path, going over at another cross-ways. Maintain direction to reach stile. Go over to leave the wood into a field. At the bottom of the field there are two oak trees: the iron gate beneath the trees gives access to a good track which soon emerges by Porch House. Turn right on

14

to the lane in Westhide village and meander around a corner to reach the beautiful **Westhide Church**.

Continue along the lane, passing a telephone box and then a half-timbered black and white building on the left. At the next corner, by Upper House, take the bridleway to the right. Go past a thatched timbered cottage on the right and then a large pond with, behind it, the buildings of Westhide farm. At a metalled drive turn left. The drive soon becomes a hard-core surfaced track and passes isolated stables, to the right and a cottage, to the left. At a three way junction, take the path which is furthest left. This meanders between woods, on the right, and open country, on the left. Ignore a left turn and carry on past a tiny pond-cum-depression on a bend. Now go uphill to reach a sharp right-hand bend: go round this, continuing uphill and so ignoring an arrowed track which goes left.

Ascend to reach a green bungalow and go round to its left. Here, an opening gives good views, left, to the Malverns and, by following a line of trees, fine views to the right are reached. There is a trig point on a mound by small trees on the left: keep following the woodland edge on the right and aim for a ruined cottage. Go downhill alongside the cottage and, after about 300 yards, reach a track coming in from the right. Turn back sharp right on this, passing some dwellings including **April Cottage** on the left. Now emerge on to a metalled lane and follow it as it descends back to the car parking space.

POINTS OF INTEREST:
Westhide Church - The church is usually closed, but it is worth trying to enter. Note the delightful bell tower on one corner.
April Cottage - This tiny, half-timbered and thatched cottage is really delectable.

REFRESHMENTS:
There are none on the walk, the nearest being in Hereford.

Walk 5   SHRAWLEY AND SHRAWLEY WOOD   3m (5km)

Maps: OS Sheets Landranger 150; Pathfinder 974.

A worthwhile and very pretty woodland walk.

Start: At 806647, as near to Shrawley Church as possible.

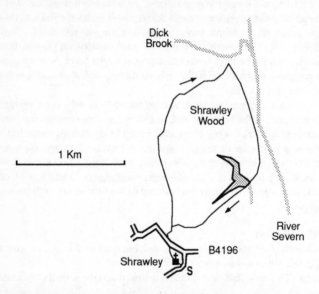

After visiting **Shrawley Church**, leave by turning right. There is a gate across the yard giving access to a path around the church boundary: follow this downhill to reach a gate to the B4196. Cross straight over and follow a driveway which leads between two detached cottages to reach a path which could be overgrown. The plant life relents after about 50 yards. Cross a stile and walk between trees. Cross another stile ahead into woodland which is predominantly oak and beech, with displays of rhododendrons in early summer. Cross a wooden bridge over a stream and bear left. A stile or adjacent gate now gives access to an open field close to Shrawley Wood House, which stands in its own grounds to the left. The ensuing clearing supports three elegant sweet chestnut trees: cross to reach another gate/stile. Continue to reach a further stile in a boundary fence. Go over and diagonally rightwards to the far left-hand corner of the field beyond to find a gate and stile which lead into woods.

16

About 50 yards into the trees there is a lake to the left. About 70 yards beyond the lake there is a Forestry Commission sign for Shrawley Wood. Here, take the left-hand of two paths, going along the edge of the wood. The path bends slightly right, back into the wood: go over at a cross-ways by a fir plantation, then over again at a green cross-roads to reach a section of secluded woodland. A track comes in from the left: continue along this, maintaining the same direction. Ignore turns to the left or right and gradually descend. About 15 yards before a wooden bridge crossing a stream (Dick Brook), look for a stile on the right. Go over this into a field and follow the edge of woodland to join up the bank of the River Severn, to the left. Go through an iron gate on to a better track, following it to reach another iron gate and stile into a meadow. After 150 yards, look for a stile in the fence to the right. Go over to reach a thin path through thick undergrowth at the edge of a wood.

Go over a rise and then dip down to reach a lake, on the right. Pass the end of this and ascend gradually on a green track at the edge of the woodland. Go through an old gate and follow a field edge towards the buildings of Court Farm. Go through the farm, by way of a gate, and continue along the same track on the edge of woods. Go over a stile and dip down rightwards on to a brown track. Go past a lake of recent origin and, about 50 yards beyond this, join the track followed on the outward journey. Now reverse the outward route back to the church.

POINTS OF INTEREST:
Shrawley Church – The church has an interesting porch and two fine wall plaques depicting the Ten Commandments.

REFRESHMENTS:
There are none in the local area, so the walker must bring his own or travel back unrefreshed.

Walk 6   FRANCHE AND HABBERLEY VALLEY   3m (5km)

Maps: OS Sheets Landranger 138; Pathfinder 953 and 952.

An encounter with two pretty valleys.

Start: At 817781, the Three Crowns and Sugarloaf Inn, Franche.

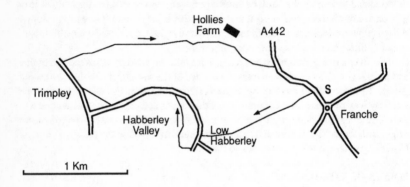

Walk north-westwards along the A442 for about 200 yards and then turn left on to a signed bridleway past bungalows to the left. On a right bend, go over the stile ahead into a field. A distinct path leads beyond an electricity pole to another stile and then to a further stile in a hedge. A path can now be seen coming in from far back on the left, while ahead there is nothing but a field of vegetables. Go left to locate a broad path across this field and, via a gap, turn right on to it. Walk towards a period farm building ahead. The Landranger sheet is unreliable hereabouts. To the right of the dwelling next to the period building, there is a gap by an iron gate. Go through and turn left on to an unmetalled lane which becomes surfaced and reaches a wider road. Go down the road to the first junction, and turn right towards Habberley Valley. Just before an old barn there is a signed track going into a thicket, to the right. Go down this to emerge in the bowl of Habberley Valley, a charming sanctuary with plenty of tree

18

cover. Turn right by a white cottage and a ranger's hut. Where the path forks, take the less distinct one, going ahead to a prominent rock (Pulpit Rock) jutting above the trees. Scramble up for a view over the valley. Keep right of some rocks ahead, go under trees and circle right of them on a path lined with tree roots. Kink right to reach a post with a red paint spot and continue to reach a little cross-roads of paths. Do not go straight on down the dip: instead, turn right on a thin path up into the trees. This trends left to reach an iron bar fence. Go over and turn left along the lane beyond. Shortly, veer left off on to a thin path which gives panoramic views over Habberley Valley and, beyond, to the Abberley Hills and the Malverns. On very good days Bredon Hill might be seen.

Continue, reaching the lane again and, after passing two houses, one either side, and a pond, left, take the signed path to the right. Go left almost immediately and follow the edge of a wood (this path is quite overgrown in summer) to reach a lane. Turn right and walk past Trimpley House an imposing Regency property to the right. Go past Trimpley Green farm, on the left, and opposite the very next driveway on the left there is a thin path: follow this into long grass and bushes to find a stile after about 50 yards. Go over and turn right, following the field hedge beyond, with a detached house to the right. Go over another stile into a more open field and walk to the first large oak tree which has a waymarking arrow. Ahead, here, there are good views of Wychbury, Clent and Lickey Hills. Now head for a line of trees, in the middle of which there is another stile, marked with a yellow band. Go over and down the next field towards three large trees, just right of which is an iron gate. Go through and walk down a sloping field, following the left fence. Go over a stile in the bottom corner and follow the stream in the dell beyond. Go over a stile and turn right along a wide track. Pass a sandstone cliff on the left, with the remains of old cliff dwellings, and then bear right with the track to reach a stile by an iron gate. Cross and go left along a green path in a field. This path gives a pretty valley walk, almost a coombe in character, passing sandstone cliffs, left, and a copse, right. Go over a stile by two bungalows to reach the A442 and go right, with care, back into Franche.

REFRESHMENTS:
The Three Crowns and Sugarloaf Inn, Franche.

Walk 7   **WYRE FOREST (ROUTE 1)**   3m (5km)

Maps: OS Sheets Landranger 138; Pathfinder 952.

Some of the pleasant woodland walking this area has to offer.

Start: At 746783, the car park on the B4194.

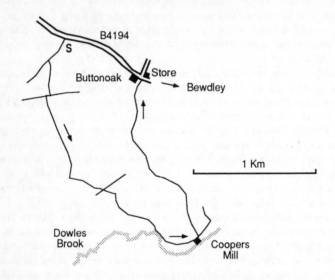

Leave the car park along the forestry track and gradually ascend into the mainly deciduous woods. About 100 yards beyond a trail branching right by a red marked post, look carefully for a track bearing left. There is a red arrow marked on a tree close by. Follow the track to reach a very broad green ride and exactly opposite carry on into fir trees. Continue most pleasantly through a mixture of larch, oak and silver birch trees, descending slightly to where a track splits off left. Ignore this left turn and go straight on, with possible sightings of deer that regularly frequent this neck of the woods. Keep descending, ignoring any left turns until a T-junction is reached, the way ahead being barred by firs. Turn left and, after about 100 yards another track, swinging in from the left, is met. Turn right on this to walk through thinner woodland, mainly oak and small firs, carpeted by heather. Swing round to the left to find a track bearing right. This leads into a small cutting with a recently cleared section of forest and a deer fence. Continue along the track, descending to reach a crossing track. Here, a right turn and a walk of about 50 yards will bring you to a bridge over the Dowles Brook. This is a delightful spot, excellent for a short break. There is a Nature Reserve in the meadow on the right.

Retrace your steps to the main track and turn right. Walk past Coopers Mill, an outdoor recreation centre. Just a few yards beyond it there are two options. The first takes the line of the stream to the left, crosses it and then follows a thin path on its left side, never straying more than 50 yards or so away. The path almost gets lost, but very soon reaches a track which loops down over the stream from the right.

The second alternative goes beyond the stream after the outdoor centre to reach a major track which loops leftwards uphill into the forest. Continue along this track for about 900 yards, ignoring a track to the left, to reach a cross-roads of tracks. The track to the left swings left and then right, passes a left turn and then loops round to cross the culverted stream and to join the first alternative. The first alternative is shorter, but harder going under foot. The second is longer but on easy tracks.

Now continue to a T-junction and branch right. Near a field ahead the track splits. Go left here to reach refreshments at the Button Oak Inn or go rightwards to reach a gate and stile that lead up to the side of some cottages and so to the B4194. Turn left to walk past a general store and continue along the road to return to the car park.

POINTS OF INTEREST:
The natural history – flora, fauna and insect life – in the forest is fascinating.

REFRESHMENTS:
The Button Oak Inn, just off the route.
The store on the B4194 also offers possibilities, although there is no seating.

Walk 8   WASELEY COUNTRY PARK $3^1/_2$m ($5^1/_2$km)

Maps: OS Sheets Landranger 139; Pathfinder 953.

A walk with superb views of Birmingham and the rural counties westward.

Start: At 972783, the Waseley Country Park Visitor Centre.

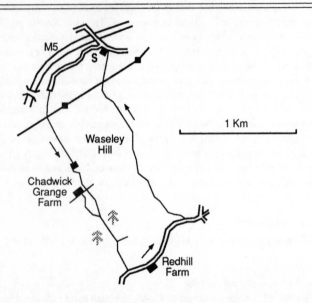

Go out of the car park and turn left along the road. In a few yards turn left into Chapmans Hill, a 'No Through Road'. This lane, hedge-rowed and lined with a few oaks either side, ascends slightly and then dips. There is no visual disturbance, but the roar of the M5, in a cutting to the right, can be heard. Continue to descend, passing, on the left, a track which forms part of the North Worcestershire Path. At a junction where a sign states 'The Cottage', bear left, the lane now widening near to a few dwellings. At this point the views stretch out over the lower lands of Worcestershire towards the Malverns. At a farm, the lane degenerates into a track: immediately go left, noting a dated signpost for Chadwich and Bristol Road topped with the National Trust insignia. Follow the track, trending left as it tunnels beneath the tree cover. The path narrows and crosses what may be a tiny brook or a larger stream, depending on recent rainfall. When a gate with a stile to the left is reached, ignore the latter and carry straight on to enter the Chadwich Estate. Here holly trees border the route: go through a gate and pass a white rendered cottage to the left. Now go across a concrete drive and through an iron gate. Keep straight on, with the M5 clearly seen about 400 yards away to the right. As the track bends round to the right to enter the grange, cross a stile ahead with a sign saying 'Footpath only, no cyclists allowed'. Go across a field towards the corner of a wood, but 50 yards down from this go over a stile into the wood. There is another National Trust sign here. The walk through the beech wood is very pleasant, a stile finally giving access to the concrete drive from the grange/farm. Follow this all the way to a lane.

Turn left up the lane, passing Redhill Farm, to the right, and some other properties before noting St Oswalds Camp set back to the right. Now go immediately left at a set back signpost (Hereford/Worcester Countryside Service) for Waseley Hills Country Park. Go to the left of a clump of trees and follow waymark arrows that lead uphill and past a notice board. Go through a gap in a fence and take a breather on the bench beyond while you admire the view over the south-western suburbs of Birmingham and catch a glimpse of the city centre some 9 miles away. Now carry on uphill to reach some stunted oak and hawthorn trees lining the route. It is clear now that these hills act as a divider between much that is suburbia and much, in the other direction, which is countryside, the latter spread for miles to the west and south. Clear visibility may allow you to see the Black Mountains of Breconshire, beyond Abberley and Woodbury Hills, the Clees, the Clents in front and as far north as Mow Cop in Staffordshire. It is also possible to see hills in Leicestershire and Northamptonshire, Edge Hill, and part of the Cotswolds. The Malverns complete the panorama, which is recorded on a toposcope on the green open hill. The only blot on the landscape is the line of pylons which cross the hills. Now, reluctantly, descend to the car park and Visitor Centre.

POINTS OF INTEREST:
The best parts of this walk are the excellent views of city and countryside from the open hills.

REFRESHMENTS:
There is a café at the Visitor Centre.

Walk 9   HOLLYBUSH AND RAGGED STONE HILL   4m (6½km)
Maps: OS Sheets Landranger 150; Pathfinder 1041.

The south end of the Malvern Hills is quiet, very scenic and demands coverage.

Start: At 759369, the car park on the north side of the A438 at Hollybush.

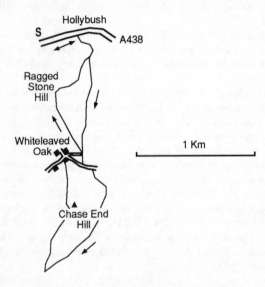

There are obvious connections of this walk with the British Camp/Eastnor Park walk (Walk 48).

Go eastwards along the A438, with great care, and just before a phone box turn right on to a track which bends left and heads uphill. At the first gate go straight on, keeping to a level path through pleasant woods. After some distance, descend through thicker woods to reach a small green with a garage opposite and a cottage to the right. Take a thin path on the left-side of the garage going over a stile in a fence and down beside a wall. Go through trees and then drop steeply to reach a lane. Turn left and, after 40 yards, turn right along a hedged track which winds steadily upwards, improving as it does. Go through a further section of woodland and then through a gate. About

200 yards beyond the gate the main path swings right. Here, carry on though a gate with path to its left as a guide. Continue ahead to reach another gate. Go through and turn right along an obvious track which goes uphill past a slab signed 'No wheeled vehicles'. Ascend directly to the summit and trig point of Chase End Hill and pause to admire the all round views. In particular, note Eastnor Castle to the left (west).

From the top of this open hill do not be tempted to go straight down. Instead, head leftwards to reach a steep green track. Descend along the track which, when it becomes enclosed, may be muddy. Go past the half-timbered Cider Mill Cottage, to the right, and turn right on to the lane by the cottages known as Whiteleaved Oak, a serene haven. Note, also, Bumble Hole Cottage across to the left. Stay on the lane, but take the next wide track bearing left, following it to reach the outward route again, close to the cottage and garage. Now, strike uphill quite steeply to gain a ridge, the way opening out and passing Malvernian granite outcrops to reach the summit of **Ragged Stone Hill**, actually a twin top. Further fine views are found here, with glimpses of the main Malvern ridge ahead. Go across to the slightly lower top and descend from it alongside a wood (Winter Coombe) to meet the outward route. Turn left and retrace your steps back to the car park.

POINTS OF INTEREST:

Ragged Stone Hill – The hill is supposedly cursed by a monk from nearby Little Malvern Priory. Against his vows of chastity, he fell in love with a local lass. The prior ordered him to crawl on his hands and knees up Ragged Stone Hill each day to pray. This led him to curse the hill and all on whom its shadow should fall. Supposed victims of this curse include Cardinal Wolsey and William Huskisson who was killed at the testing of Stephenson's Rocket.

REFRESHMENTS:

There are none on the walk, but there is an inn, *The Duke of York*, at Rye Street, two miles to the east along the A438.

Walk 10   BRINGSTY COMMON CIRCUIT   4m (6$\frac{1}{2}$km)

Maps: OS Sheets Landranger 149; Pathfinder 995.

An excellent example of a heathland common.

Start: At 698551, the picnic area/car park off the A44.

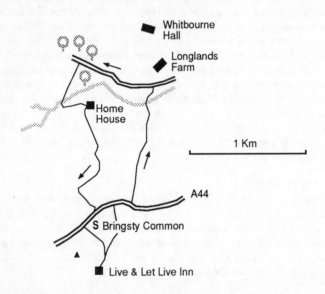

Walk beside the A44 across the unfenced common, heading eastwards and passing a derelict chapel on the right. Turn left across the common on a good track opposite, and some yards beyond, the chapel. This track goes down to a corner stile which is crossed into a field. Trend left across the field to reach another stile. Go over and follow the general depression of a valley, with views opening up towards Whitbourne Hall ahead.

Go through a gate and head straight on to reach a footbridge on the left. Cross and go through a gate on the right to reach a track. Follow the track uphill to reach a metalled lane. Turn left along the lane, noting Longlands Farm, to the right, and, behind it, **Whitbourne Hall**, just visible among the trees which surround it. Continue along the lane, passing a coppice, to the left, and then walking along one to the right.

Turn left at the sign for Old Mill Cottage. It is now necessary to take a route which bends round left in an orchard to reach Home House, with a hedge on the right. Go through a gate by the house and cross the yard to reach a gate on the right. Go through into another orchard. Climb a bank and, just beyond a gap, go over a stile into the next field. Walk along the field's right hedgerow to reach another gap, with a hedge to the right, to reach a stile below an ancient oak tree. Cross and follow a thin green path bordered with holly which goes between cottages and out on to the common. The centre of several green tracks is now followed to a road. To return to the start, head straight for the picnic area.

But for refreshments, take the track signed for **The Live and Let Live Inn**. Go past a farm and an orchard on the right and continue for about 400 yards to reach the Inn. From it, retrace your steps, then take the first track on the right which climbs steeply between bracken. Head back for the road and take the short walk back to the picnic area.

POINTS OF INTEREST:
Whitbourne Hall – The hall was the work of the architect Elmslie and was built in 1860.
The Live and Let Live Inn - This fine old inn, built of stone and half-timbered, was originally a cider house.

REFRESHMENTS:
The Live and Let Live Inn, close to the route.
There is also a café at Bringsty garage further along the A44.

Walk 11   HANBURY AND BIRMINGHAM CANAL   4m (6½km)

Maps: OS Sheets Landranger 150; Pathfinder 974.
A Church, a Stately residence and a Canal.
Start: At 959649, Pipers Wood, on the B4091.

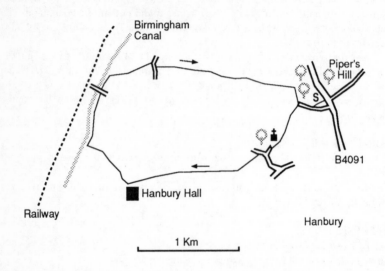

Walk south along the road and turn right on to a narrow metalled drive. Walk past a drive, to the left, and cottages, to the right, to reach two footpath signs, one of which points towards Hanbury Church, seen on its hilltop. Go through a kissing gate, (waymarked with an arrow) and walk towards the church. Climb up and go through kissing gate with a small wood, to the right. A third kissing gate leads into the cemetery. Go past the church of St Mary the Virgin and exit through the church gate on to a lane. Pass a cottage, to the right, and at a parting of lanes another footpath sign guides you straight across on to National Trust property. These are the grounds of **Hanbury Hall**. Cross the field on a distinct route with glimpses of Hanbury Hall in the distance. Eventually, you will reach a small pond situated by a metalled road and, over the brow of a hill, another pond. Walk directly across the field ahead, aiming towards a small wood. Cross a waymarked stile into the next field. Now ignore the stile to the right and walk close the field's fenced perimeter. Continue with a wood to the left to reach a gate into a farm. On approaching the buildings a small humpback bridge will be seen. This crosses the Birmingham Canal, beyond which is a railway line. A simple gate, just a piece of wood really, gives access to a short descent to the canal. Head north-north-east along the canal towpath, passing two sets of lock gates, the second of which lies just beyond another hump-back bridge which carries a lane. The footpath goes over a stile to leave the canal. Cross a small bridge over a stream and cross several fields, linked by stiles, to reach a lane. Cross and go over the stile in the hedgerow opposite.

You will now be able to see Pipers Hill: the route now heads for this wooded lump. Keep close to the left side of a field and go through a gate. Note Webbhouse Farm over on the right, a useful landmark. Cross another stile on to the lane to the farm. Cross and go over another stile to walk across a field which can be muddy. Go over two stiles which straddle a little stream to reach the next green pasture. More stiles and green enclosures, and another crossing of a tiny stream on a miniature bridge brings the walker to Pipers Hill. Here the farmer has recently erected a metal gate and wire netting. If this is still there it must be crossed to reach a wood. Go rightwards, through the wood, to reach a cottage and an opening on to a semi-metalled lane. Go left to reach the B4091 and the start of the walk.

POINTS OF INTEREST:

Hanbury Hall - This fine Wren-style hall was built in the last years of the 17th century and houses a fine collection of porcelain. The Hall is owned by the National Trust and is open for the standard Trust hours.

REFRESHMENTS:

There are none on the walk, but cream teas are available at Hanbury Hall and there is a choice of inns within a short distance.

Walk 12   **WYRE FOREST FROM CALLOW HILL**   4m (6½km)

Maps: OS Sheets Landranger 138; Pathfinder 952.

Lovely walking in mainly deciduous woodland.

Start: At 743738, Callow Hill car park, just west, and opposite, the Forester Inn.

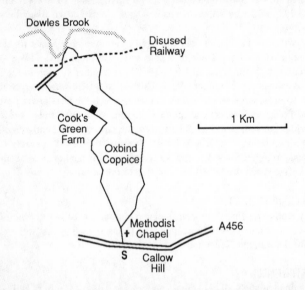

Before starting the walk be sure to admire the nearby **church**. Now walk down the vehicular drive and go left towards the signed 'Rose Bine Cottage Only' path. The path crosses a stile: keep the cottage to the left to reach a wood. There is a sign here, noting 'Footpath Only, Horses Keep Out.' Go into the wood ignoring a small path to the left to find a more obvious track to the left. Follow this track through oak woods to reach a small track coming in from the right. Take this down to a stile and cross a small stream by way of a thin plank. Turn immediately right and walk past some fine silver birch trees. Swing left to meet a broad track and there go over a stile immediately to the left. Cross over another path by signs warning 'Private Property, Keep Out', then swing round right to reach a stile by an iron gate. Ahead is a sign on a tree, 'Sheep Area, Dogs must be kept on Leads': kink round by a stile and go over two

30

planks across a stream. Now walk up alongside a fence and some electricity cables. There is a property standing back leftwards: go over a stile to the right, then go left, then right again to go through an iron gate. Keep to the edge of the open field beyond, following the edge of a wood on the left, and walk down to reach a post near a tiny stream. Here there is an arrowed stile to the left.

Go over the stile and, immediately beyond, go over another to the right. The stile gives access to a tiny metalled lane. Go right. Walk past a post and a walking sign and, after another 100 yards, follow a track ahead noting the signed 'Private Road, Footpath Only' sign on a tree. A gate leads to a cottage made of local stone: walk around its boundary to meet a brook which is either crossed direct or by way of a wooden bridge. Beyond the brook a path coming in from the left is met. Take this as it swings rightwards with the Dowles Brook below on the left. Now begin a long loop to the right to meet the track of a former railway. Turn left and walk along the old track to reach a major forestry track crossing ahead. Turn right up the forestry track. Just after a left-hand bend, there are two signs for 'Callow Hill Car Park'. Ignore the one to the left, carrying straight on and passing several benches. Now look to the right-hand side of the track to see a blue arrow pointing right. Take the indicated path, then turn left to walk alongside some fir trees, with a field some yards to the right. Keep straight on, as directed by two arrows on a post, with the field still to the right. When you emerge by a group of shacks, follow the hard-core drive to return to the Wesleyan chapel and the car park.

POINTS OF INTEREST:
Church - This Methodist church was built in 1864 as a Wesleyan chapel.

REFRESHMENTS:
The Forester Inn, at the start.
There is also a store on the A456 about $^1/_2$ mile west of Callow Hill.

THE LICKEY HILLS 4m (6½km)
or 7m (11km)

Maps: OS Sheets Landranger 139; Pathfinder 954.
Despite the urban fringe, these are lovely hills.
Start: At 986758, the Beacon Hill car park.

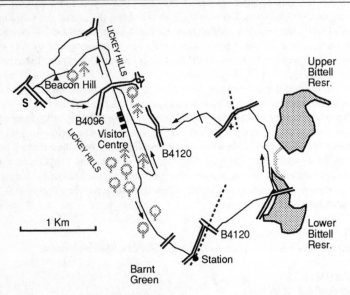

From the car park walk out on to the level grass which lies at over 900 feet (around 275 m) above sea level. Bear right around a holly bush and go through a gap in the hedge beyond. Go right and then swing left on to a good track. At a cross-ways go ahead on a stepped way to reach a T-junction. Turn left, and then take a steep staircase into a wooded valley, going over a small stream. Turn left on a good path by a picnic area, to the right, and landscaped pools, to the left. Cross over one pool's edge and approach the Rose and Crown Inn before joining the main B4096. Go left, with care, then cross to reach the first path on the right. This good path flanks the base of a hill, to the left, passing the **Lickey Hills** Nursing Home to reach a Visitor Centre. Behind this there is a small play area, beyond which there is a good track. After about 600 yards the track splits.

For the shorter route, take the left fork, going under steep slopes, to the left, decked with conifers. Now, on a bend, go uphill on a stepped path. The hill crest is easily gained and good views open up to the right. Walk past a strange cast iron contraption and continue to reach a car park.

The longer route goes straight ahead at the fork. Go past a shelter to reach a T-junction by wooden railings. Turn right on a broad track which ascends and curves left through deciduous woodland. Pass another shelter, to the right, and soon reach a lane. Go left for 10 yards and then take the track opposite going through beeches and then between houses set back on either side to arrive opposite Barnt Green Railway Station. Turn left and walk to the B4120. Turn right, go under a bridge and then turn first left into Margesson Drive. Go round Barnt Green Sports Club at the end and then go over a stile in a passage alongside the building. Cross two fields, the second by going diagonally right, to reach a lane. There are good views of Lower Bittell **Reservoir** from here. From the lane turn first left along a bridleway to reach a small stretch of water. Here, take a short excursion to the right, over a stile, to see Upper Bittell Reservoir. Return to the main path, which is now metalled, and go past Tower House, to the right. Turn left at a T-junction and go under a railway bridge. Walk past a church, to the left, and then take the signed North Worcestershire Path, reached over a stile, along a wood edge. Continue along a field edge, then turn left at a post and cross two stiles in quick succession. Cross a long field to reach houses and the B4120. Cross and climb up opposite to reach the shorter walk at the car park.

Go over the hill crest, passing heather borders and silver birch, then, at rocky outcrops, descend steeply on a stepped path to the B4096. Cross and turn right along a bridleway fringing a golf course. Ascend a hill, descending its far side to reach suburbia's edge. Now either keep to the course's right edge or aim directly for Beacon Hill. Each option will soon lead you back to the starting car park.

POINTS OF INTEREST:
Lickey Hills - Although the Hills lie within Worcestershire, the area is administered by the City of Birmingham. The Visitor Centre has some interesting exhibits on the area.
Reservoirs - The two Bittell Reservoirs are a haven for numerous species of waterfowl.

There are fine views and excellent mixed woodland all along this route.

REFRESHMENTS:
The Old Rose and Crown Inn, on the route.
Refreshments are also available at the Visitor Centre.

Walk 15 WYTHALL AND WEATHEROAK HILL 4m (6$\frac{1}{2}$km)

Maps: OS Sheets Landranger 139; Pathfinder 954.

An attractive pocket of rolling countryside between three major roads.

Start: At 075752, the corner of Chapel Lane, Wythall.

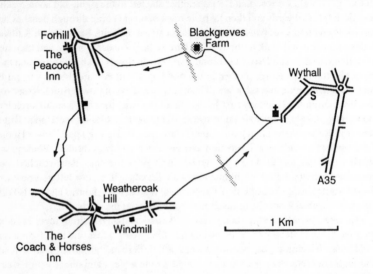

From a car space either in front of, or opposite, Wythall Cemetery, walk along Chapel Lane to reach Wythall church. On the bend just beyond, turn right on to a waymarked drive, passing farm sheds and some prefabricated bungalows behind the right boundary. Follow the boundary round to the right to where fields open up. Go over a stile in a hedge on to a golf course. Follow the right-hand edge of this to its far boundary fence and then swing left, keeping with the boundary until a right turn is made over a ditch, by way of a plank with a stile beyond. Ahead is the attractive Blackgreves Farm, the main house surrounded by a water-filled moat. Go diagonally right over a small enclosure, then over a stile by the outbuildings and cross an attractive stream over a small bridge. Go along the right hedgerow of the field beyond to reach a gap waymarked by an arrow. Keep straight on, ignoring a leftwards path at this point. A further right-

34

hand field boundary is now followed, by way of a gap into a field which appears to give split paths. Take the one bearing slightly right to reach a North Worcestershire Path post. Go under the trees and turn right up a lane. Just before the 'Give way' sign, turn left on the North Worcestershire Path, going through a picnic site by toilets to emerge opposite the Peacock Inn.

The North Worcestershire Path continues along Lea End Lane, but we leave it, turning left along **Icknield Street**. Follow this as far as Mount Pleasant Farm, to the left. Some yards beyond this, and opposite, look carefully for a stile set back in the hedge. Go over and follow the edge of the field beyond to reach a corner and thicket where there is a stile into the next field. There are fine views to the right, of the Lickey Hills across a sprawling valley, but the M42's traffic noise carries easily to here! Steps and a further stile give a steeper descent along the left field edge to reach a lane. On this descent there are fine views of rolling hills ahead. Turn left along the lane, and go left again at a T-junction. Admire the half-timbered Weatheroak Farm, to the right and continue to reach the Coach and Horses Inn and the Weatheroak Restaurant adjacent to it.

From the Inn, ascend Weatheroak Hill by road. Go past Millfield Cottage, to the right, and note the disused windmill in the adjacent field. Go over at a cross-roads and walk past Hall Farm, to the left. Turn left over a stile by a gate beyond this and head for another stile across the small field beyond. There is a good view of the bell tower of **Wythall church** from here. The field edge reaches a footbridge over a stream: if the next field is ploughed, follow its left boundary, swinging right to reach a gap and post. Follow the field path beyond back to Chapel Lane.

POINTS OF INTEREST:
Icknield Street - The Street, which is shown as Ryknild Street on the OS map, is a Roman road.
Wythall church - St Mary's Church, Wythall, though relatively modern, has a striking and architecturally interesting bell tower.

REFRESHMENTS:
The Peacock Inn, Forhill.
The Coach and Horses Inn, Weatheroak.

Walks 16 & 17   LEDBURY AND FRITH WOOD   4m (6½km)
or 8m (13km)

Maps: OS Sheets Landranger 149 & 150; Pathfinder 1041 & 1018.
An historic English town, fine woodland and an open hill.
Start: At 711377, the car park behind St Katherine's Hospital,
Ledbury.

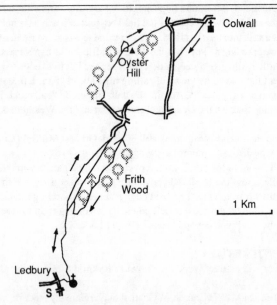

Walk out to the High Street, from where the car park is signed, and cross by the
17th-century timbered Market House to enter the delectable Church Lane. Cross the
small cobble stones between historic buildings to reach the grounds of St Michael's
Church. There is a red brick period building on the left and along its far side an
alleyway: take this through to a lane, bearing right by the John Masefield High School
to reach some steps ahead. Enter a wood with houses on the left. Emerge on to a
metalled lane via steps and take the public footpath opposite. At the first left bend,
take the hard-core-cum-metalled track which leads into Frith Wood House and
continues beyond. Soon, a track leaves the main one, going left into a field. Follow
waymark arrows which give a general line along a woodland edge. Cross a cottage

garden and go through an orchard, keeping to its right-hand side to note the multi-arched railway viaduct over the River Leadon. Go past a house and join the drive to Frith Farm. Now follow a signed path, right, which opens out to reach a lane.

The shorter route returns through Frith Wood from here, the route being given later in the text.

For the longer walk, turn left up the lane, passing a path to the right which is noted for future reference. Pass some buildings to reach a Victorian house and a lane, going right, signed for Hope End Hotel. Here there is a footpath leading up a field diagonally left towards trees: take this, continuing past the far side of an enclosure with greenhouses/nursery. Follow the edge of the trees to reach a fenced path and climb this to the trig. point of Oyster Hill, a fine spot for a rest and to admire the view.

From the summit descend a thin track into a thicket of trees. Cross a sandy red track and go over a rough brow ahead to reach a stile into a pasture, with West Malvern and North Hill prominent ahead. Keep an iron fence to your right to reach two close stiles into a wood. Beyond little steps give access to an open field. Go through a copse on a thin path and cross a field to reach a lane. Turn right by the solitary house, then go left towards Colwall with its fine church and adjacent ale house.

From the church car park, go diagonally across a field towards the stout oak. Beyond, in a corner, there is a footbridge: go over into the next field, walk along its boundary and then go slightly right to reach a stile in the hedge. Go over and cross the next field aiming for an oak to reach a lane just beyond the house on the far side. Go down the lane for $\frac{1}{2}$ mile, then look carefully for an innocuous path between two houses opposite the next road junction for Colwall. The path heads through trees and goes left of large iron gates to reach an iron gate/stile. Go over and cross the field beyond following the right-hand hedge. Enter and exit a small portion of woodland and cross a field to reach a lateral track. Cross this and follow a boundary fence over a brow to emerge on to the lane followed earlier. Reverse the outward route to reach the path into Frith Wood. Here we rejoin the shorter route.

Take the far path uphill into woodland, going through a gate, to reach a bend on a wider track. Now maintain a straight route uphill through young trees to reach an open crest with views of May Hill and the Cotswolds, to the left. The path continues into higher woodland, then descends abruptly to reach a kind of T-junction. Go right here, almost doubling back for several hundred yards. The descent leads down to a wide forestry track. Turn left and follow this to Frith Wood House from where the outward route is retraced back into Ledbury.

REFRESHMENTS:
All tastes are catered for in the fine historic town of Ledbury.

Walk 18   NEWNHAM AND KNIGHTON ON TEME   4¹/₂m (7km)

Maps: OS Sheets Landranger 138; Pathfinder 973.

A decent couple of hours or so in quiet countryside, with a fine Norman church.

Start: At 643694, the Tavern Inn, Newnham.

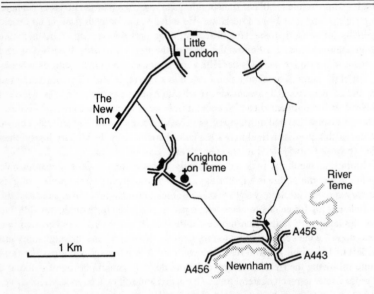

Exactly opposite the entrance to the huge car park of the Tavern Inn is a gate signed Oxnall's Farm. Go through and follow a hard-core drive which, after a short distance, swings right by a pylon towards the farm. Do not follow it: instead, go on through an iron gate and follow a green track hugging the hedgerow. In about 200 yards, two gates appear: take the left-hand one, beyond which a thin track crosses a strip of trees and hedgerow. A possibly overgrown path section is then navigated to reach a good track beyond a gate. Continue to a T-junction where a bridleway sign points right. Here, go left on a broad track. Walk past a large farm complex on the left and continue on a metalled surface passing three dwellings, two of which are half-timbered. At a T-junction, turn left for 50 yards, then go right through an iron gate on to a vehicular way at the field edge. This trends left under small cables, giving views of Titterstone

Clee Hill. Beyond the cables, at the second gap to the right, is an iron gate. Go through and turn left along the field edge where a thin track may be discernible through sandy soil. Go past a large isolated dwelling, partially timbered, on the left, and after a further 100 yards look for an inconspicuous gate on the left. Go through and hug the right-hand boundary to reach a concealed stile by a telegraph pole. Go over on to a lane and turn left, noting the tiny, timbered Homelea Cottage on the left. Turn right, signed Tenbury, to cross an area known as Knighton Common. Here you can walk all the way to the New Inn for refreshments, or turn left 250 yards before it at a sign in the hedgerow.

The signed track edges a static caravan site and then traverses a copse to reach a stile into an open field. Head across the field towards some open barns. There is a farm building tucked away to the left, but the walk swings right away from this on a track. Now go down a rough field for some yards and then through the first gap in the left-hand hedge. Undulate past two conspicuous oaks maintaining direction to reach an iron stile in the far boundary. Turn right on the lane beyond and walk to a cross-roads. Turn left on a lane signed for Knighton Church. Pass the parish rooms and the Old Rectory on the left, then go through a white gate on to a lane signed for Church Farm. When this swings left, go through the lych gate to inspect the beautiful **church of St Michael and All Angels**. The keys can be obtained at Newnham Post Office.

Opposite the lych gate, across the lane, there is a public footpath to Newnham: take this, trending diagonally left to reach an iron gate in the far left dip. Beyond this, swing left through another iron gate and then go right, along an elongated field passing under pylon lines. At the truncated end of the field there is a wooden gate. Go through into the next field and follow a hedge to another gate, on the left, on to a metalled drive. Follow this lane, passing dwellings to emerge back at the Tavern Inn.

POINTS OF INTEREST:

Church of St Michael and All Angels - The church is in the parish of Lindridge and has the same vicars listed as that of Lindridge Church. The tower is cedar-shingled and dates from only 1959! The narrow south entrance is Norman. The nave was built in the early 12th century, while the nave roof is 15th century. The chancel arch was built in 1120, though the chancel itself is 14th century. A complete guide to the church is available from the post office.

REFRESHMENTS:

The Tavern, at the start/end of the walk.
The New Inn, Knighton Common.
There is also a general store in Newnham.

Walk 19   WHITNEY-ON-WYE AND BRILLEY   4½m (7km)

Maps: OS Sheets Landranger 148; Pathfinder 1016.

Pretty country walking above the Wye Valley.

Start: At 267475, near Whitney Church.

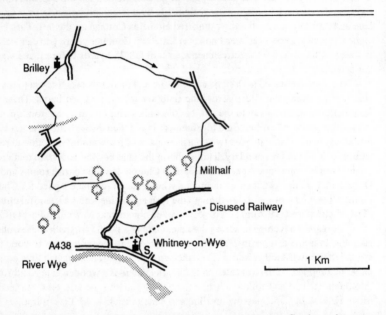

Brilley

Millhalf

Disused Railway

A438

Whitney-on-Wye

River Wye

S

1 Km

Follow a drive alongside **Whitney church** to reach an iron gate. Go through on to a
public footpath which crosses a field and soon goes over a footbridge over an old
railway. Turn left at the gate beyond and walk up through woodland to reach the
period Whitney Court, to the right. The fenced path reaches a kissing gate: go through
and walk up a lane, passing a proud half-timbered dwelling. Continue as far as a gate
and footpath sign to the right. Just up and opposite this is a gate into the wood on the
left. Go through and follow a thin path through the wood to reach a T-junction with a
gate beyond. Go through into a field and head rightwards towards the tall trees. Go
over a stile into the wood and curve round to reach a bigger path. A gate has been
barbed-wired here, so keep to the main track, to the left, to find - care is needed - a
thin track going sharp right. Take this to a wooden gate with a sign advising 'You are
being watched!' Go through and, shortly go through a white gate, to the right, with a

re-directed path sign on it. Now go left on a muddy track to reach a footpath sign between cottages. Go straight on, then cross a lane to reach a signed track. When the track bends left, take the path between the trees to the right. Cross a stream by footbridge and head up a hedged gully path. Ignore a junction on the right, continuing along the waymarked vehicular track. Where this forks, look carefully up the bank to the right and use steps and a stile to reach a field. Cross this and another field, using waymarked stiles, to reach **Brilley church**.

From the churchyard go out to the lane seen ahead. Walk past a telephone box and a new bungalow, to the right. About 100 yards further on, a re-routed path goes over a stile to the right. Swap hedge sides by way of a gate/stile: there are good views of the Black Mountains to the right here. Swap hedge sides again, as waymarked, and go through a boggy gully to reach an isolated house whose drive is followed to a lane. Go ahead, passing a right turn, to reach a T-junction. Turn right. After about 100 yards, beyond a cottage to the right, turn right on a signed green path and descend to a stream ford. Slog up the other side, cross a lane and go over a stile into a field. Trend downhill and rightwards, with a poplar plantation to the right. Pass a cottage on the left and then turn right on to a small metalled lane. After 400 yards turn left over a stile and bear right by a stout oak tree to go over a plank across a tiny ditch. Head for the far woodland boundary and follow it, with Whitney Court coming into view. Further along, an arrow points to a gate. Go through on to a path along a fence to regain the footbridge used on the outward route. Now retrace the outward route back to the start.

POINTS OF INTEREST:

Whitney church – The first village church was destroyed when the Wye changed its course in 1720. The present building dates from 1740 and was built by Mr Wardour, the squire. The wooden altar swept away by the river was recovered from the river at Hay on Wye. It is now in the old church at Hay.

Brilley church – St Mary's Church is 13th to early 14th century, but with a modern tower built 1912 to replace the original which had burned down in 1910. Inside there is a 12th century font.

REFRESHMENTS:
The Boat Inn, Whitney-on-Wye.
The Rhydspence Inn, Rhydspence, west along the A438.

Walk 20 AYMESTREY AND MERE HILL WOOD 4¹/₂m (7km)

Maps: OS Sheets Landranger 137, 148 or 149; Pathfinder 972.
Though not shown with rights of way, Mere Hill Wood is Forestry Commission and there are no problems with access.
Start: At 425654, the Crown Inn, Aymestrey.

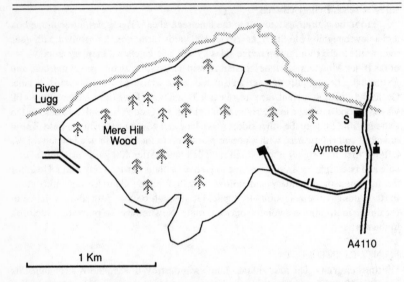

On the A4110 there is a road bridge over the River Lugg and on its south bank, nearest to the town, there is an excellent track heading left into the woods. Take this, passing under limestone crags high up on the left. There is a limestone quarry here which can be explored: it may even be of interest to climbers!

Back on the route, what has been deciduous tree cover now becomes conifer, with several good examples of Douglas Fir. The aim is to keep near the River Lugg, which necessitates a left fork and soon a right one to regain the river. Now follow the river for about 1 mile, a most pleasant interlude, before trending away from it at a gate. Bear left to again walk below limestone quarries. Ascend to a gate and go through it, following a woodland edge with Covenhope Valley on the right. The River Lugg once flowed down here, but was cut by a blockage during the Ice Age. Glacial meltwater forced its new course which has been followed ever since.

There are two sharp intrusional corners in the forest and the path circumnavigates these, reaching the apex of the second where the main path (as previously walked) must be left in favour of a smaller one which goes uphill through the trees to emerge in open country. Keep the field boundary on your left hand at first, then go through a gate and walk with the boundary on your right. The way ahead is undefined, but crosses a broad gentle slope aiming for the edge of another wood. To the right there are fine views over the flatlands near Leominster.

Follow the woodland edge to reach a lane. The right of way is shown as crossing this, proceeding to a building and then following a drive into Aymestrey. However, this is not good walking and it is better to use the lane to descend to the main A4110 in Aymestrey. On the way, be sure to visit the **Church of St John and St Alkmund**, before returning to the Crown Inn.

POINTS OF INTEREST:
Church of St John and St Alkmund - The church, which has a most unusual dedication, is worth visiting for its beautiful 16th century screens.

REFRESHMENTS:
The Crown Inn, Aymestrey.

Walk 21   STOKE LACY AND LITTLE COWARNE   4½m (7km)

Maps: OS Sheets Landranger 149; Pathfinder 994, 995, 1017 and 1018.

A pleasant ramble through rolling hills and a good valley to finish.

Start: At 621494, Stoke Lacy Church, off the main A465.

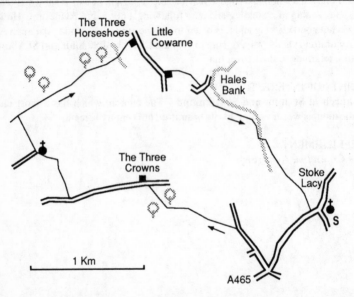

Walk south-west, with care, down the A465 for just under ½ mile and turn right at a lane signed for Little Cowarne. Walk along the lane to an ivy clad tree on the right. Opposite is a gap and a gate: go through the gap into a field and follow its left-hand hedge. Where this turns left at a corner, carry on to locate a gate into the next field. Go diagonally right on an undefined course across this field and then follow the hedge up to an iron gate. Turn left through the gate and walk alongside the edge of a wood for about 100 yards to reach a small corner where there is a gap through the trees/hedges. Go through and ascend over the open, domed field to reach an iron gate beyond which a lane is reached opposite the Three Crowns Inn. Turn left down the lane. Go beyond a drive with a walkway sign for a further 100 yards and look carefully for an iron-topped stile to the right. Go through and walk across the pasture beyond, heading towards Ullingswick and its church. Go through an awkward iron gate in a hedge to reach an orchard and cross it towards a house, keeping close to the right boundary to reach a gate on to a lane. The actual right of way is confusing on this section and could, alternatively, go leftwards to reach a wooden gate and so emerge on to the lane between buildings. Either way, go left to **St Luke's Church, Ullingswick**.

Turn left away from the church for 10 yards, then turn right along a drive to reach a T-junction near a corrugated barn. Turn right. Two iron gates at each end of a pasture now give access to a wood. Follow its edge, climbing along the field boundary. There are extensive views to the right and behind on this section, May Hill, Skirrid Fawr, Sugar Loaf and the Black Mountains being visible. Carry on at a crossing of ways to go over a brow by a cottage, left. Descend to reach the modern Three Horseshoes Inn. Go right from the inn to find a walkway sign and driveway, to the left. Go past a bungalow, to the left, and then through gates and fields. When a pair of gates is reached be sure to go through the left-hand one. Beyond this wooden gate, go down the field edge to reach a stile (of sorts) close to an isolated property. From the property's garden follow the drive to reach a cottage with a barn and garages. The right of way goes through these to reach a walkway sign on a tiny lane. Go towards the cottage ahead and then hug the right-hand boundary fence to reach a gate to the other side of the fence. Pass via a hawthorn hedge to join the bank of a stream. Cross a broad bridge to the left and then go over a wooden bridge in a nice valley situation. Turn right and follow the boundary round to find a stile and bridge into a pasture. Walk past a red brick dwelling on the left and go through a gate on to a drive. Follow the drive to emerges on to the main road. Turn left to return to **Stoke Lacy church**.

POINTS OF INTEREST:

St Luke's Church, Ullingswick - St Luke's Church is 12th century in origin, two small round-headed windows in the nave dating from this period. The chancel was restored in 1856, the rest of the church in 1862-3, the restoration accounting for the present bell turret, porch, nave roof and pews. Note the memorial to John Hill on the wall, whose children died in infancy.

Stoke Lacy church - St Peter & St Paul Church has Norman origins, the earliest rector being John of Bristol in 1279. Of the six bells the tenor dates from about 1400 and was cast by the Worcester Foundry. The church was restored in 1863.

REFRESHMENTS:
The Three Horseshoes, Little Cowarne.
The Three Crowns, on the route.

THE MALVERN HILLS $4\frac{1}{2}$m (7km)
or 9m ($14\frac{1}{2}$km)

Maps: OS Sheets Landranger 150; Pathfinder 1018.
Mainly on imposing hills, but also two interesting side tracks.
Start: At 766472, the verge of the B4232.

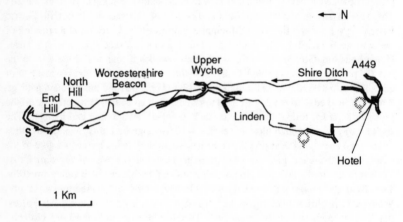

These routes take the northern and middle sections of the **Malvern Hills**.

On the bend in the B4232, take a rising path near a stone tablet signed 'No wheeled vehicles, Penalty £20.00'. Go up through trees to reach a switchback after about 300 yards. Now either contour round, or ascend, End Hill, continuing towards North Hill on obvious paths which go past a bench overlooking Great Malvern. A diagonal track finds a col between Table Hill and North Hill. You may climb North Hill if you wish by going about 100 yards steeply uphill to the left. Return to the col and use paths to climb Worcestershire Beacon. Note the toposcope and then descend the natural ridge. Now either use a metalled track or gain it later, thus keeping to the skyline along the ancient Shire Ditch to reach the car park at Wyche Crest where there are white houses to the right.

The shorter route returns from here, walkers needing to locate a wide track bearing left at the top end of the car park. A further description is given later.

For the longer route, from **the Wyche**, take a right fork and descend to Upper Colwall. At the hairpin bend take a metalled footpath between firs. This bends right near Linden Manor at whose gates you should take a green hedgerowed ride which skirts the Manor. Swing further right near a field edge, the way being undefined but leading to a depressed track on the left. Now follow a coppice line, noting a barn 50 yards to the left. Continue along the trees and hedges and then go right through two iron gates to reach a track. Turn left on a lane past Upper House, then bear right by it, noting the Malthouse. Cross a field to a corner and then swing left and right along the edge. Go over a stile and cross a stream by way of a wooden bridge. Go over another stile and climb up the field beyond to reach a stile at the top. Go past a newish brick building to emerge on to a road by the Malvern Hills Hotel. From here, head north along the B4232. Choose any of several ways back on to the ridge to traverse Black Hill (South and North), Pinnacle Hill and Perseverance Hill to regain the Wyche by way of twisting steps leading downhill. The shorter route is rejoined here.

Go up the car park and bear left on the wide level track and descend to reach a road at a bus stop. Strike uphill again in a few yards to find a metalled drive into a car park beneath the steep sides of Worcestershire Beacon. At a higher car park by a disused quarry, three ways present themselves. Take the middle one, by small conifers, and follow it to an open common, passing two benches. Follow the boundary wall of a property, then ascend rightwards up a valley side. Almost at the col, switchback left around the valley head and contour the slopes beyond. Do not descend yet: instead, continue on a green track, ignoring a fork to the right. Keep low past a curious stone monument under a tree, then bear left at the next fork, going through an iron gate by an extended house and descending steeply to a lane. It is a short step to the B4232: turn right to return to the starting point.

POINTS OF INTEREST:
Malvern Hills - Under the jurisdiction of the Malvern Hills Conservators. Worcestershire Beacon has outcrops of Malvernian Granite over 600 million years old. The hills rise quite suddenly out of the Severn Plain. They are over 6 miles long but very narrow, only $^3/_4$ mile between the roads on either side.
The Wyche - The cutting is on an ancient salt route.

REFRESHMENTS:
The Malvern Hills Hotel, on the longer route.
For both routes there are numerous possibilities in Great Malvern.

Walk 24   SUTTON ST NICHOLAS AND MARDEN   5m (8km)

Maps: OS Sheets Landranger 149; Pathfinder 1017.
A flat walk, near the Lugg Valley, and a small hill.
Start: At 534454, Sutton St Nicholas church.

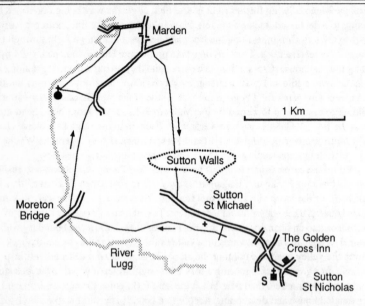

From the church, which has an attractive porch, go left along a lane to reach a cross-roads. Go straight over, on a road signed for Marden, soon crossing straight over at another cross-roads. Walk past Ordis Cottage, a fine black and white half-timbered house on the left and, just beyond, turn left on to a signed public footpath. Follow this path (initially a hard-core drive) to reach a signed stile on the right. Go over and cross a field to a waymarked stile. Go over and cross a (possibly cropped) field to reach the next waymarked stile. Cross and head towards the left-hand corner of a farm. Go beyond this by way of a couple of gaps to meet a leat, but where the fence that bounds this bears rightwards, divert leftwards across a large field to reach a stile in a fence, just left of a stout oak. Take a middle course across the next large pasture to reach an iron gate and stile on to a lane near the River Lugg. Turn right, but immediately go left over a stile into a pasture close to the River Lugg, on the left. Soon, veer away from the river to reach a stile in a fence. Cross and walk to another stile, going over and crossing the field beyond. At a gate, bear slightly right towards a visible junction sign near two white houses, reaching the sign by way of a stile in the corner. Turn left for **Marden church.**

Leave the church along the footpath in the north corner of the churchyard, by the edge of a garden. Continue across river meadows to reach the 17th century bridge at Marden, keeping the river close except at one bend where it loops away. Turn right into Marden village. Go right again at a junction (Walker's Green) and walk to a T-junction and a sign for Paradise Green. Turn left and, after 150 yards, go right through a gate on to a public footpath which runs along the field edge. Kink left and right over a stile to reach the other side of the hedge. Go over two further stiles to return to the other side of the hedge. Continue to reach a line of trees where a stile gives access to **Sutton Walls**, the earthworks being rather hidden by undergrowth and trees. Go straight on over the hill on a thin path through a copse to reach a concrete drive. Continue in the same direction, going downhill on the concrete drive to reach a cottage and a lane. Turn left along the lane, soon noting Sutton St. Michael's little Norman **church** on the right. Now simply continue back into Sutton St Nicholas retracing the outward route back to the start point.

POINTS OF INTEREST:

Marden church - The church is isolated from the village, as a result, it is said, of a meeting between King Offa, whose palace was at Sutton Walls, and Ethelbert, King of East Anglia, to discuss a marriage between Ethelbert and Offa's daughter. Offa, recognising a little late, that the marriage would increase Ethelbert's already considerable power, had the latter murdered and his body buried by the river. During the burial a strange light filled the sky. Offa, fearing divine retribution, tried to repent by giving a tenth of his property to the church and also went to Rome on a pilgrimage. The Pope told him to build a church on the site of Ethelbert's grave. The present church is a later building, but occupies the same site.

Sutton Walls - The earthworks of Sutton Walls date from the Iron Age. The site covers 28 acres and is now thought to have contained a complete settlement within its fortifications.

Sutton St Michael church - The church contains two fonts. One is Norman, the other is 17th century.

REFRESHMENTS:

The Golden Cross Inn, Sutton St Nicholas.
There are also possibilities in Marden.

Maps: OS Sheets Landranger 138; Pathfinder 952.
Pleasant hilly woods and riverside scenery.
Start: At 790741, a hard-core car park on B4194 close to the
River Severn.

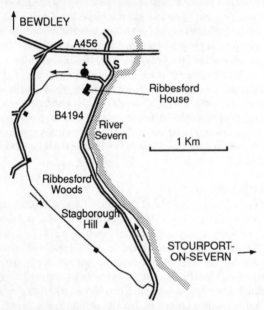

From the car park, where there is room for several vehicles, proceed southwards along
the B4194 for about 250 yards to reach a sign, pointing right, for Ribbesford church.
Take the signed metalled lane, which is lined mainly with horse chestnut trees, and
note the attractive facade of Ribbesford House across the field to the left. The lane
leads towards buildings almost hidden beneath thicker trees and then opens out into
something of a small square. Ignore everything to the left and turn right, soon noting
a wooden signpost saying 'Main Route'. This is part of the Worcestershire Way and
will take you to the churchyard of **Ribbesford church**. Go either way round the church,
then proceed uphill to reach a stile in a corner. From here there is a very fine - and by
far the best - view of the church. Waymark arrows now point out the route which goes

across a field and into a wood. Keep close to the right boundary on the steady, but leafy and pleasant, climb through the wood to reach a house to the right. Beyond this the track improves and leads to a metalled lane. Turn left along the lane passing the buildings of Horsehill Farm. Beyond, there are fine views over the woods towards the Clent Hills, Romsley Hill, Waseley Hills and the Lickeys, with part of Kidderminster and Stourport seen in the middle distance.

Where the lane bends sharp right, take a track to the left just beyond a detached house. This leads very pleasantly through Ribbesford Woods. Ignore all turns to the left and after $^3/_4$ mile leave the wood by going into an open field. Ignore the exact reading of the Landranger map and take the cart track through the middle of the field, going through a green gate and staying left of the map route and a ruined cottage. Though not the marked route, this is the obvious way and has the option of allowing a detour uphill to the trig. point on top of Stagborough Hill. Descend and swing left either just beyond some trees or further right to reach the B4194. Turn left, with care, along the road and, in under $^1/_2$ mile look for a step stile to the right. Go over and back on yourself for some yards to pick up the river path (which is being improved at the time of writing). The route currently follows the edge of a beet field, with high Himalayan Balsam lining the right of the thin path in late summer. Keep close to the riverside as the path improves. Note the Woodman Inn, to the left on the B4194 , which is joined for the final walk back to the starting car park.

POINTS OF INTEREST:
Ribbesford Church - The church is a fine sandstone building of Norman origin supporting a wooden steeple, which is most unusual for this district.

REFRESHMENTS:
The Woodman Inn, on the B4194
All tastes are catered for in Bewdley which is only 2 minutes away by car.

Maps: OS sheets Landranger 138; Pathfinder 953.
A very attractive canal section to this walk.
Start: At 832792, the Lock Inn on the B4189.

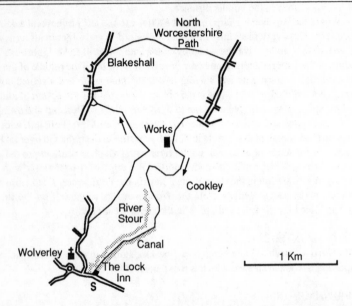

Leave the large car park of the Lock Inn and head west along the B4189 almost to the
island at junction of B4190. Just before reaching this island, take the narrow, one-
way lane which turns very acutely right (It has a weight limit sign at its beginning).
Go past the church of St John the Baptist, Wolverley, or enter the church grounds to
find a nice viewpoint of **Wolverley** village. Now walk down the very narrow lane
with sandstone cliffs on the left, passing quaint white cottages as the lane snakes
down into the village. Walk past the Queens Head Inn, on the left, and note the
Courthouse, dated 1620. Walk up the lane between cliffs, passing the Live and Let
Live Inn set back on the right. Soon, take the lane called the Short Yard - a 'No
Through Road' - which bears right. Beyond the last dwelling, walk past a modern
farm outbuilding on a bridleway, ignoring a right bend. Carry straight on into a line of
mixed trees and then go over a stile at the end. Go along the left edge of the field

beyond to reach a sharp dip. At the bottom of the valley to the left, aim for a waymarked wooden stile. Go over and follow a thin path which climbs obviously through a grass field, goes through a gap and crosses a second field, going under electric cables. Head for the buildings ahead passing these to reach a gate-cum-stile on to a lane. Turn right, following the sign for Kinver.

Within 400 yards a path goes right into a thicket. This can be used as a shorter variant of the walk, following the path to meet a lane, crossing it and then descending steeply to reach a wide track which is taken, to the right, along the River Stour.

However, the walk described here ignores this path, continuing to reach a bridleway and then bearing right to meet the North Worcestershire Path which descends pleasantly through fields giving open views towards the Clent Hills. Follow electricity cables on the obvious path and go past brick built barns and an isolated dwelling with landscaped gardens on the left. On reaching a lane at a junction, turn right and follow it to another junction. Go over, then turn right as the lane bends round and right again up a hard-core drive signed 'West Midlands Equitation Centre'. After about 250/300 yards you will see a thin path coming in from the trees on the right, by a telegraph pole. This is the shorter version of the walk. Take the next available left turn to cross a bridge over the River Stour. Now walk close to factories, bending right beyond to reach the towpath of the **Shropshire and Worcestershire Canal**. Turn right to follow the canal in most pleasant surrounds. A canal side dwelling, two locks and a footbridge are passed after which the towpaths opens out from leafy glades a little, before heading back into sylvan surroundings, sometimes with small sandstone cliffs lining the opposite bank. A fine white house is passed across the water, followed shortly by another dwelling set back a little on the same bank. Eventually the towpath reaches locks and the Lock Inn starting point, to the left.

POINTS OF INTEREST:

Wolverley - a pleasant village containing the Courthouse, dated 1620.
Shropshire and Worcestershire Canal - one of the prettiest canal towpaths in the region.

REFRESHMENTS:

The Lock Inn, at the start.
The Queens Head, Wolverley.
The Live and Let Live Inn, Wolverley.

Maps: OS Sheets Landranger 150; Pathfinder 1043.

*Where Worcestershire meets the Cotswolds, the village and the
escarpment make a fine walk.*

Start: At 095374, the car park off Church Close, Broadway.

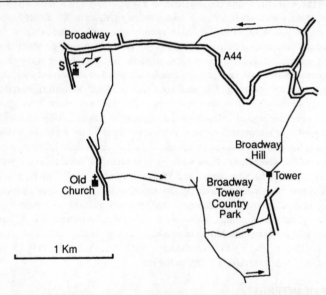

It is worthwhile starting the walk by visiting the fine church of St Michael and All
Angels built in 1839. Return via Church Close, passing the car park and a veterinary
surgery to the right, and take a footpath into trees. Swing left and right and go over a
stile. Go past the Campden Bakery and bear left and right into Broadway's main
street. Walk past an open field and the Horse and Hound Inn opposite, and then look
immediately right for a signed path that takes an alley to the recreation ground and the
old church. The alley leads to a field strip: go over a stile and cross a field, going
under cables, to reach another stile and a tiny stream. Further fields and waymarked
stiles lead to a kissing gate in a corner. Go through and turn left along a lane to **St
Eadburgha's Church** (Broadway's old church). Opposite are two Cotswold stone
gate portals and a footpath sign. Take the wide path through trees, gradually ascending

54

to a point just short of a T-junction and horse jump. Turn right here, going over a stile and through a gate, then heading upwards with fine views out right. Pass an isolated bungalow and soon reach 'Door Knap', with its multi-gable ends, down and to the right. A corner offers two options: turn left and go uphill, passing two houses, on the left, to meet a metalled lane. Before this reaches a junction at the top, go over a stile on the left. Now cross a ladder stile into the picnic area of Rookery Barn.

Take any one of several paths from the barn leftwards towards **Broadway Tower**. The route now goes through the National Trust site of Clump Farm, so keep on the level from the tower, going through a waymarked gate behind it and contouring the hill in a fine position. The Cotswold Way goes left and downhill into Broadway from here, but our walk continues through a waymarked gap in a drystone wall. Cross an open pasture, going into a slight dip and following a waymarked post to enter a wood. Where the path splits, bear right to reach the main A44. Directly opposite is a Cotswold Way sign: take the path going down and left of this. Go through trees and up steps on the right to reach a little track going off left. Take this, passing two large beech trees and keeping near the edge of the wood on the right. The ground falls away sharply to the left into the wood: look for a path twisting down left and take this to a lane junction. Opposite is a signed footpath: take this, going over a stile and downhill towards Broadway. Head down a rough pasture aiming just to the right of three large trees in the hedge boundary ahead. Go over a waymarked double stile and aim for a prominent ash tree. Go to the left of the tree and walk along a hawthorn hedgerow to reach a defined track. This soon gives way to a grassier path which leads to an iron gate with a wooden gate and stile to its left. The thin path beyond follows iron railings to meet the main road which is followed, with great care, back into **Broadway**.

POINTS OF INTEREST:
St Eadburgha's Church – The old town church - the parish church until 1849 - was built in about 1200. The saint of the dedication was King Alfred's granddaughter. Inside are the arms of King Charles I, these having been rescued at the time of the Civil War and saved by the Savage family. They were placed in the church in 1773.
Broadway Tower – The tower was built by James Wyatt, in 1779, for the 6th Earl of Coventry. It was possibly used as a signal tower and once housed the manuscripts of Sir Thomas Phillipps.
Broadway - There is much to see in the town, best of all, perhaps, being the Teddy Bear Museum passed at the end of the walk.

REFRESHMENTS:
There are choices for all tastes and pockets in Broadway.

Walk 28   ROMSLEY HILL AND WALTON HILL   5m (8km)

Maps: OS Sheets Landranger 139; Pathfinder 953.

A worthwhile addition to walking in the Clent Hills area.

Start: At 943802, Walton Hill car park.

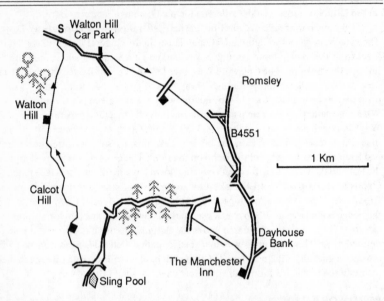

Proceed along the lane beneath Walton Hill and take a left fork to go down to the first farm buildings. There, go over a stile at a footpath sign and cross fields down to a lane, noting fine views of the Black Country skyline and seeing a glimpse of Birmingham. Go left along the lane, then immediately right over a stile to follow a signed footpath for Romsley Hill. The footpath may be muddy at first, but improves as you climb away towards two prominent trees and then make for the top left-hand field corner adjacent to back gardens of houses in Dark Lane, Romsley. Hidden by a holly hedge is a stile: cross and go through trees to reach open land and fine views of Walton Hill and Adams Hill. Kink round through a gap and then go straight on, keeping the radio mast at Romsley ahead, to reach a lane by a footpath sign and iron gate. Cross the green ahead and proceed down the B4551, using its left grass verge, to reach the Manchester Inn. Just before the inn there is a stile into a field: go over and climb up towards a wood. Keep to the edge of the wood, with it on your left hand, following a well-defined track which is part of the North Worcestershire Way. A succession of fields with waymarked stiles lead obviously towards houses and a lane. Turn right up the lane for 150 yards, then go left into Winwood Heath Road. Go past prefabricated houses and then dip steeply through trees, perhaps with glimpses of Walton Hill across a deep valley. Although the lane has a metalled surface, the descent gets easier as it approaches a tree-filled valley. After swinging sharp right by a dwelling, turn left into Shut Mill Lane leaving the North Worcestershire Path behind for a worthwhile excursion to Sling Pool, a National Trust site cradled in a lovely dell and abundant in waterfowl and aquatic life.

Retrace your steps to the cross-roads and take the 'No Through Road' noting the bridleway sign. There is a division in the ways in a few yards: the concrete drive to the right states that it offers no right of way, so go left of the dwellings to where a footpath sign points to Walton Pool on the right. This merely regains the concrete drive a few yards further uphill, a most curious diversion (!). On the skyline ahead is Calcot Farm: reach its perimeter wall and locate a stile straight ahead. Beneath it is a rock from the Arenig Mountains, North Wales, brought here by the last great Ice Age. Go over the stile and follow the perimeter fence, bearing right to reach a stile in a hedge. Go left over this: you are now following the Clent Hills Circuit route in reverse (Walk 52). It is worthy of a reverse outing for its scenic value, the views seen from a different aspect. Pass the bench presented by the Wednesday Wanderers Rambling Club and walk through Turkey Oaks on the obvious edge of the hill, with splendid valley overlooks right. Romsley Hill and the woods lining Winwood Heath Road are seen. Pass another bench dedicated to Betty and Ron Gardiner, then go over two stiles and turn left, as waymarked, by a cottage. Take the wide track to the right and walk towards the firs cresting Walton Hill. Pass a North Worcestershire Path post and then the trig point. Continue along the broad ridge, but turn left after about 50 yards to go down a diagonal track which leads back to Walton Hill car park.

POINTS OF INTEREST:
The undulating countryside on this walk is a joy throughout, as are the superb views at almost every turn.

REFRESHMENTS:
The Manchester Inn, on the route.
There is a kiosk at the Walton Hill car park.

Walk 29   INKBERROW AND DORMSTON   5m (8km)

Maps: OS Sheets Landranger 150; Pathfinder 996 and 997.

Very open and flat walking, if you like this sort of thing.

Start: At 015573, the Village Green, Inkberrow.

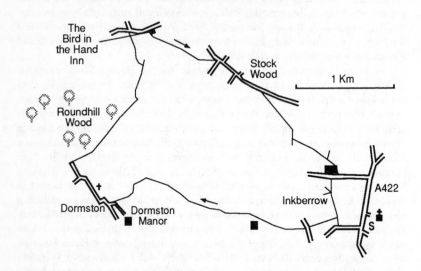

Turn left from the village green to walk down to Stonepit Lane. Turn right into the estate, passing a road to the right. After about 150 yards turn right on to a signed path. Go past a modern barn, left, and by its left edge follow a wide track into a field. Follow its left edge into a gully between houses, cross a lane and follow the signed path opposite towards Dormston. Go over a stile and into a small field. Go over an awkward stile, then half-right to another awkward corner stile. Go through a hedge gap and soon return to the same field over a stile. Turn left along this long field aiming for a large tree beyond electricity cables. Go over a stile and walk along the left hedgerow of the field beyond to reach an iron gate in the left-hand corner. Cross the middle of the next field, go through two iron gates and cross a track. A thin path is discernible across the next field: follow it to a gap in the hedge. Go through a gate, over a ditch and turn immediately left. Go through another gate on the right and cross a field towards a cluster of white houses. To the left is Dormston Manor, with superb chimney pots. By a white cottage, a gate gives access to a lane. Go right to visit **St Nicholas Church, Dormston**. Beyond the church, the last of the houses is Orchard Cottage, with unusual modern dormer windows. Beyond this go through a gate on the right and follow the edge of a wood. Switch sides of the hedge, by way of a gate, then change sides again. Suddenly the hedgerow ends and the way seems lost: take a central line across a field and trend left towards the end of the wood on the left. Now go down the wood edge and around a field, trending right to reach an innocuous gap in a hedge. Go left through this, kink left and then go straight on, along a line of trees. At a lateral line of trees, go slightly left to find a stile into a field. Keep to the field's left edge and exit through a gate on to a lane. Go right to reach the Bird in Hand Inn.

Facing the inn, to the right is a footpath: take this and go past Woodlea on a drive and green avenue. Ignore a stile ahead: instead go over a stile 20 yards to the right, by a wooden bridge. Go over and walk right, around the field beyond to reach a stile in a hedge. Go over, turn left and follow a hedge to a trough-cum-stile. Ignore this and trend right along the field edge to reach a black and white building. Beyond is a wooden bridge which leads left by a copse. There is a modern white cottage to the right and a stile ahead: go over and turn left along a lane to a T-junction. Turn right, pass Stockwood Lane, to the right, and Stockwood Thatch, a partly thatched cottage, to the left, to reach a footpath sign for Inkberrow. Go diagonally left and up a field to reach a large oak tree in a corner. Go over two awkward stiles and continue to reach a double stile almost at the end of the next field. Cross it to reach another double stile near a brook and bridge. Go diagonally right towards the large farm buildings behind trees. Go through a gate and head for the top left corner of a field and so reach the farm complex. Zig-zag through gates and buildings and cross a lane to reach a gate. Go through and keep to the hedge on the right to reach a stile on the right. Go over and turn left to reach a stile at the backs of houses on the modern estate in Inkberrow. To the left is a stile into the estate: go over into Windmill Lane and wind round before turning left and left again to return to the village green.

POINTS OF INTEREST:
St Nicholas Church, Dormston - The church is beautiful with its half-timbered tower and old wooden porch. It is usually closed, for access tel: 0386 792591.

REFRESHMENTS:
The Bird in Hand Inn, Stock Green.

Walk 30   PERSHORE AND TIDDESLEY WOODS   5m (8km)

Maps: OS Sheets Landranger 150; Pathfinder 1019.

A period town, a fine abbey, woodland and riverside make for an excellent walk.

Start: At 949457, in Pershore.

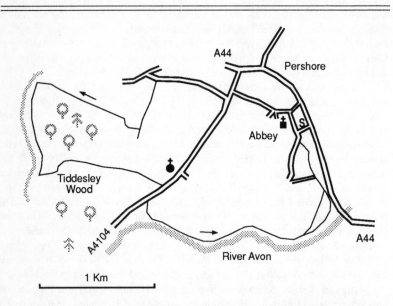

Before starting out, please check the parking restrictions where you have left your vehicle.

Begin by walking along Defford Street, then turn right for **Pershore Abbey** and go into its grounds. After a good look at the ruins, go across to a black and white gable end. This is the Almonry. Go along the street known as Newlands passing period terrace cottages and the Talbot and Victoria Inns. Turn left at the T-junction and go first right into Holloway. This opens out beyond the last house, to the left, and you turn left at the second major drive, on to a public footpath. Pass a ruin with a modern barn behind and walk to a waymarked post beyond another ruin. Bredon Hill dominates the view ahead, while the Malverns can be seen to the right. Now turn right and circumnavigate a wood following the waymarking arrows and going over several marked stiles. Go right, then left, around the edge, traversing fairly flat, but pleasant, open country. Cross a track and enter the woodland. Follow a path down and exit the wood by steps. Go left along a green path along the wood edge, with a fine brook, lined with willows, flowing to the right. Go left over a waymarked stile into the wood again and, in a few yards, turn left at a T-junction. Now maintain direction all the way through the wood, following the blue arrow waymarks.

Enter a field by way of a gate/stile and, in the second field, aim for a thatched cottage and a gate waymarked with a blue arrow. Go through and follow the metalled drive beyond to the A4104. Turn right, with great care, for 200 yards, then go left by a walkway sign, going over a waymarked stile and bearing right into a field. Although the right of way is shown going away from Pershore, it is best to turn down the left hedgerow and then to go left across a wooden bridge over a stream. Now follow the banks of the River Avon for about 1 mile . Before the A44 road bridge is reached, bear left and follow metal rails or, indeed, leave the river's edge in the final meadow to gain the same place. Find a gate/stile in the hedge and go up an alleyway of hedgerows. Cross a cycle track into a paved alley with playing field to the left. Turn right at the top and then go left into a curving street at the backs of two-storey, terraced houses. This will lead you back into **Pershore** and the start of the walk.

POINTS OF INTEREST:

Pershore Abbey – Built of warm yellow Cotswold stone and with a surviving 14th-century tower, though much was destroyed after the Dissolution. For what does remain we have to thank the townsfolk who saved it to use as their church.

Pershore - This important historical town has many fine 17th- and 18th-century buildings.

REFRESHMENTS:

All tastes are catered for in Pershore.

Walk 31 STANFORD BRIDGE AND SAPEY COMMON 5m (8km)

Maps: OS Sheets Landranger 138; Pathfinder 973.
A delectable walk in lovely surroundings - hilly and wooded.
Start: At 715658, the Bridge Inn, Stanford Bridge.

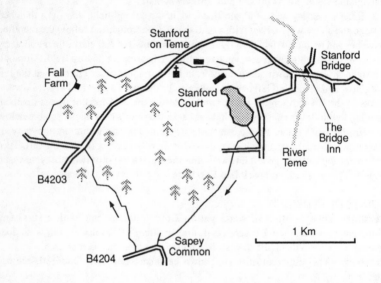

Leave the Inn's car park by crossing the old bridge over the River Teme 'Rebuilt by Worcestershire County Council in 1905'. Cross the B4203 into a lane signed for Shelsley Walsh. Walk ¹/₂ mile, going around a sharp bend, to where a drive can be seen off right in a dip ahead. There is a stile here, close at hand on the right: go over into a small field and cross to reach another stile on to a hard-core drive. Go over this and another stile and cross the field beyond to reach an iron gate. Go left over a stream, with a cottage on the right. A gate-cum-stile gives access to a drive: cross to an iron gate and a waymarked post. A good track climbs the field edge beyond to reach an iron gate and, beyond, a waymarked post inside a wood. Attack the hill direct and, sure enough, a thin track leads up through the wood to reach a stile into a field. Follow the edge of the wood to reach a gate beyond which a track follows the right-hand edge of the next field. Sapey Common's houses are ahead now: a gap leads to a lane at a house, opposite, called The Benbows. Go left to reach the B4204 and turn right along it. Go past a nursery, to the right, and at the end of some poplars and a hedge you will reach a little drive with a gate, on the right. Take this to reach another gate and go through on to a track that goes left, then right. Looking ahead beyond the first portion of forest there is a dwelling in a clearing which can be used as a guide. Veer left at the next gate into a good pasture and walk down to an iron gate into a wood. The good track beyond gives a lovely wooded interlude as you walk along the edge of the wood to reach a stream crossing bearing right. Now bear left under electric cables to reach a gate and cross the B4203 into a lane.

Follow the lane for some distance, then turn right along a drive signed for Fall Farm. Go left before the farmyard, following a track down to a bridge. Just beyond is a gate, to the right, with a blue arrow waymark: go through into a wood and follow a thin bridleway, pleasantly trending downhill to reach open land by a red-brick dwelling. Continue along a drive to emerge at the Old Schoolhouse at Stanford on Teme. At an angle opposite on the main road there is a walkway sign. It is possible to go uphill to inspect **St Mary's Church, Stanford on Teme**. Retrace your steps downhill towards old barns, going over a couple of stiles. Go through an iron gate and a large pasture with Stanford Court, now used as a timber yard and sawmill, on the right. Go through an iron gate in the lateral boundary fence ahead and trend right to find a wooden stile on to the metalled drive leading away from Stanford Court. Walk along this and go right at the B4203 to the start point, again going over the old bridge.

POINTS OF INTEREST:
St Mary's Church, Stanford on Teme – The churchyard has a superb display of daffodils in the spring and swallows nest above the inner door. Despite the mess, this is rightly encouraged. The door key can be obtained from Grayham Tate at the Old Schoolhouse.

REFRESHMENTS:
The Bridge Inn, at the start, or the attached café/shop.

Walk 32   **LINGEN AND HARLEY'S MOUNTAIN**   5m (8km)
Maps: OS Sheets Landranger 137; Pathfinder 971 and 972.
Quiet, with a good valley and a broad hilltop with fine surrounding views.
Start: At 366670, the Royal George Inn, Lingen.

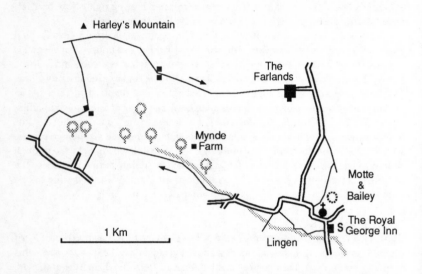

This walk could be linked with Walk 84 for a strenuous day out.

From the Royal George Inn, walk south for 50 yards and then turn right by a footpath sign. Almost immediately, enter the grounds of a white cottage and walk by the brook in the garden, crossing it over a wooden bridge. Go through a gully and over a stile into a field. Keep close to the fence on the right and go through a gate into the next field. Go right, cross the nearby wooden bridge, go over a double stile and bear rightwards across a pasture to reach the gate seen ahead. Turn left on to a lane at a bend and, about 50 yards beyond a sign on the right saying 'No Footpath', take a little lane going uphill to the right. Go up to reach a telegraph pole with a walking sign, near a gate and an old ruin. Turn right through some trees to reach another gate with an adjacent stile. Go over and walk through an avenue of hawthorns, with a

64

stream below on the right. A fence-cum-stile gives access to a very pretty valley: keep on a line a few yards above the stream as there is no trace of the right of way shown bearing right on the OS map. You will arrive at a fence and thick hedge, again with no trace of a through way: veer steeply uphill to the left to reach a wooden fence which can be used as a stile to gain a lane. Turn left and follow the lane, passing a bridleway to the right, all the way to a junction with another lane which services some isolated dwellings.

Turn right and follow this new lane past a large detached dwelling with a pink gable, to the right, and two dwellings, to the left, to reach 'The Red House', a white cottage on the right. Exactly opposite this there is a gap by a tree and small fir: turn left through the gap and, soon after, go through a gate and climb steadily uphill through an avenue of trees. Some distance up this, the farmer has blocked the path with barbed wire across, but, fortunately, this is easily bypassed. Continue, to reach a gate, to the right, waymarked with two arrows, one yellow, the other blue. This is a good spot to survey the loneliness of the situation and the view of the surrounding hills, including the Radnor Forest. Turn right through the gate and, if inclined, visit the trig. point summit of Harley's Mountain some yards away to the left. Now follow the near boundary, going through an iron gate and then another one where the hill dips away below. There are fine outlooks ahead and right from here. Bear slightly right over a field to find an iron gate on to a good track which leads to some corrugated barns in a group of pines. Continue along the track, which is now metalled, passing a small plantation, to the left, and noting Lingen nestling in the flat valley on the right. Descend via The Farlands, a farm complex, to reach a lane. Turn right and, after a few hundred yards, just beyond a bungalow and a cottage, locate a signed stile in the hedge to the left. Go over to reach a field path. Head for a gate with a stile to its left and, beyond, head for the church spire by going over a wooden bridge and several stiles. Pass the motte and bailey, to the left, and enter the **church** grounds over a stile. Exit left on to a lane and turn the corner back to the start.

POINTS OF INTEREST:
Lingen Church - This attractive church was rebuilt after a fire in 1861.

REFRESHMENTS:
The Royal George Inn, Lingen. Please note that the inn is closed on Mondays!

Walks 33 & 34   **PEMBRIDGE AND EARDISLAND**   5m (8km)
or 8¹/₂m (13¹/₂km)
Maps: OS Sheets Landranger 149; Pathfinder 993, 971 and 994.
Classic Herefordshire villages and a pastoral river valley.
Start: At 390581, the New Inn, Pembridge.

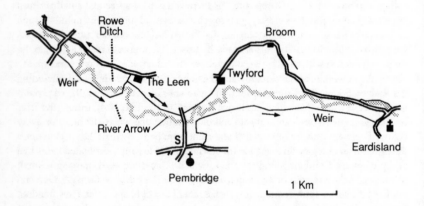

From the back of the inn, get on to the A44 towards Leominster and turn left by the almshouses (dated 1686) into a haulage yard, finding a gate on the left. Go through and cross a field to a stile and footbridge. Follow the edge of the field beyond, which bends leftwards, and go through a gate on to a green lane. Go over a stile, to the right, at the rear of houses, and walk to the next stile. Go over and turn right. The walk now follows the River Arrow, which is away to the left. Go over several stiles linking arable fields to reach the river at a weir. A cropped field could now force the walker around the field boundary and care is needed to locate a stile hidden in the hedgerow on the right. Go over, turn left and follow the field edge to another stile. Cross the meadow beyond to reach a road. Turn left into the charming village of **Eardisland**.

Pass two junctions to the right and one to the left to gain a river path, to the left, on the Arrow's northern bank. Go over a stile near what looks like an old motte, and bear left through a caravan park. Keep left to reach a road and turn right along it. The river is close by at first but is left behind as you follow the road into Broom. Continue along the road to reach Twyford. Turn left down the drive to Twyford Farm and go over a stile on the right. Trend slightly left to reach a stile. Cross a field and two further stiles to reach a road. Turn left.

The shorter walk returns to Pembridge from here by following the road over the River Arrow and back into the village.

The longer walk takes a drive to the right before the river is crossed. Go over a signed stile on the right and follow a field boundary, keeping to the right of farm buildings. Maintain the same line over the next field, go through a gate, over a stream and a stile and follow the field edge to the right into a corner. Cross a disused railway and follow the right-hand hedge. Pass a farm (The Leen) and cross its farm track and a stile opposite. Go diagonally right across two fields to reach a lane by the Rowe Ditch. If this is blocked/obstructed it might be necessary to turn right on to a lane, then left along it to reach the Rowe Ditch, a tree covered earthwork on both sides of the lane. Now follow the lane to Staunton-on-Arrow, another fine village in a superb setting. Return along the lane to reach a footbridge opposite the last house. Go over into a pasture and continue to a lane. Turn left to reach a junction. A gate opposite gives access to a stream: follow this to its junction with the River Arrow. Continue for a short way, then turn right over a waymarked stile. Follow the edge of the field beyond and then go along the river before veering away by a small plantation and a waymarked stile. Go over the stile into a field and follow its edge to a path. Follow the path to reach Leen Farm once again. Beware of footpath obstruction here. Cross the river by bridge to reach the farm and turn right to retrace your steps back to the lane near **Pembridge**. Turn right to return to the start.

POINTS OF INTEREST:

Pembridge - This superb black and white village has a glut of cruck-framed houses. There was an annual fair held here virtually continuously from 1240 to 1946, when it ceased due to traffic pressure/use of the A44! The church is 14th century with an almost pagoda-shaped detached bell tower, with a short, shingled spire.

Eardisland - The village is beautifully positioned around the River Arrow. Of particular interest is Staick House, built around 1300. Also noteworthy is the 17th century Old Manor House: its brick dovecote has 800 nesting alcoves.

REFRESHMENTS:

There are ample opportunities in both Pembridge and Eardisland.

Walk 35 TILLINGTON COMMON AND BADNAGE WOOD 5m (8km)

Maps: OS Sheets Landranger 149; Pathfinder 1017.

A spread out village, open land and a length of woodland characterise this walk.

Start: At 465454, the Bell Inn, Tillington.

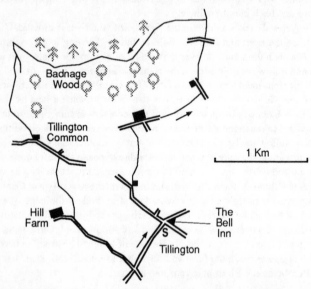

Proceed north-west along the lane from the inn, heading towards Tillington Common. Go past the first right turn and continue past Burghill and Tillington Cricket Club on the left. You will soon reach an attractive black and white farm on the right: just beyond it is a path heading right, into a field. Take this, following the near edge of the field to a stile. Go over and continue to another stile with three waymark arrows on it. Proceed ahead across a field to reach a waymarked post. Cross the next field along its right-hand edge. Towards the end of this field turn 90° left to find a stile in a hedge. Go over on to a lane and turn right. Follow the lane until it swings right and there continue ahead on a bridleway, by a stone cottage and barn to the right. A blue arrow gives the line to a green avenue of hedges and a waymarked gate leading into a field. Follow the boundary hedge, passing a shed under an oak tree to reach black barns.

Turn left on to a lane. After about 200 yards, just before a detached dwelling, follow the line of a waymarked post, to the right, into an orchard. Keep to the right-hand boundary and look carefully for a waymarker post where a hedge confronts you. Turn right along the hedge boundary on a broad track and, after 200 yards, locate a waymarker post in the hedge. This points you through a gate, across a thin lane to another gate opposite. Follow field boundaries and stiles to reach the edge of a wood where there are two stiles.

Go over the nearest stile into the wood, then go steeply uphill into the firs, crossing a plank and a waymarked stile and using steps to cross a track. A plank and further steep steps lead upwards as part of a tough ascent which levels out on the crest of the wooded hill. Further waymarker posts allow you to join a track coming in from the left. At a clearing, keep to the right-hand edge to enter further woodland. Continue straight on at a post with two arrows on it and go through a waymarked gate on the right. Now follow posts waymarked with yellow arrows until suddenly they change to blue ones. Go through a gate on the right into a field and, about 50 yards, beyond follow the line of a blue arrowed waymarker post to the left. A protracted descent now follows, going down through woods with occasional glimpses out to the right across fields to further wooded hills. Eventually, you will reach a waymarker post with both blue and yellow arrows. Follow the blue arrows to the right to emerge on a lane by Wood Cottage. Turn left along the lane to reach the first turning on the left by a post box and bungalow, on the right. Now take the diagonal path to the right, which goes over Tillington Common to reach the left side of Hill Farm and a thin metalled lane. Go left along the lane to reach a junction between two cottages. Turn left and follow the lane to the cross-roads and the Bell Inn. An alternative to this last section is to avoid the Common by simply walking the lane pleasantly back to the inn.

POINTS OF INTEREST:
This walk offers a long section of woodland walking during which many common species of bird may be observed.

REFRESHMENTS:
The Bell Inn, at the start.

Walk 36   **KILPECK AND COLES TUMP**   5½m (9km)

Maps: OS Sheets Landranger 149 or 161; Pathfinder 1064 and 1040.

A wonderful Norman church and a fine hilltop.

Start: At 446305, Kilpeck Church.

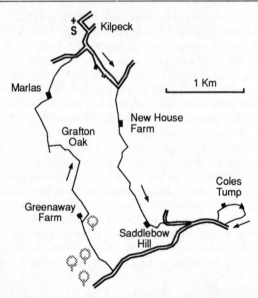

From the **church**, walk along the village lane to a T-junction. The Red Lion is opposite. Turn right, and soon bend left to where a road sign points to the village hall. Pass this, left, and climb to a T-junction. Turn right into a 'No Through Road' to New House Farm. Go straight through the farmyard from where an iron gate leads a wide track, possibly through crops. Go through a wooden gate and turn right along a field edge. Ignore a gate on the right and follow the boundary, swinging left to reach another gate. Follow the green track beyond, with a ditch and low hedge on the left. Go through a gate and field to reach a squat oak. Follow the left-hand hedge beyond to a gate, beyond which there is a good track between trees. A large wooden gate gives access to a yard by a farmhouse: take the little drive left and snake round to a lane. Join another lane and head for **Coles Tump** with its distinctive crown of trees. After a few yards, go left through a gate by a bungalow. Turn right and climb hill by any route. Go over a stile in the fence beyond and cross rough pasture to a fence beyond which is the trig point summit of Orcop Hill. Turn right and walk down to a gate. Go through, turn right and retrace your steps along the base of the hill to the lane.

Bear left and follow a lane along the base of Saddlebow Hill, passing a group of houses. Just before reaching a stone cottage and attached barn, there are metal gates on either side of the lane. Go through the right pair and along the right field edge to a hedge gap. Trend leftwards to a gateway in the middle of the next hedge and go straight across another field to cross a fence on to a farm track. Walk towards the farm to reach a stile on the right, just before the barns. Go over and bear left to follow a fence down a field. A gate leads to a diagonally left descent which reaches a stream where a hedge on the far side reaches it. Go through a gate and cross the stream on stepping stones. Go along a hedge to reach a gate into a pasture. Cross this into another. Trend leftwards over another field to reach a green lane and follow it past Grafton Oak and on to a metalled track. Turn right and descend to cross a brook. Go right, over a stile and a small enclosure. Now keep to the right-hand hedge and cross a fence just right of some conifers. Walk along the stream on the right, go through trees to cross a footbridge and continue to a green lane. On reaching a metalled surface, go over a stile on the right and cross a field to its far left corner. There, cross a footbridge and stile into another field. Keep to the left edge of two further fields, go past a house and walk along a hedge to reach a gate on to a lane. Turn right to return to Kilpeck.

POINTS OF INTEREST:
Kilpeck Church - The church was built in 1140 and is almost entirely Norman. Note especially the semi-circular apse and the ornate carving around the main door. A decorated corbel table runs along each wall with many representations of mythical beasts. The font is very ancient and probably pre-dates the church.

Coles Tump - The tump is dotted with flat-topped earthworks called 'pillow mounds', apparently constructed by the Normans to encourage rabbits to breed, rabbits being a Norman delicacy! From the top the view includes Skirrid Fawr, Abergavenny Sugar Loaf, the Black Mountains, Hergest Ridge, northern Herefordshire, Aconbury Hill, the Forest of Dean and Garway Hill

REFRESHMENTS:
The Red Lion, Kilpeck.

Walk 37   TWO WYE VILLAGES $5^1/_2$m (9km)

Maps: OS Sheets Landranger 149; Pathfinder 1016.

Mainly flat with one excellent viewpoint and some extensive orchards.

Start: At 365452, the New Inn, Staunton on Wye.

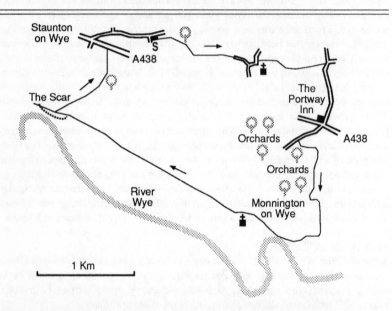

There is a public footpath alongside the inn's car park: take this, passing a bungalow and going over a stile into an orchard. There all traces of path disappear (!), so turn left along the boundary hedge and, in 100 yards or so, go diagonally right through the trees to reach a boundary hedge with a detached red-brick house behind. Go over a stile into a field and follow vehicular tracks near the hedge on the right. Just beyond two solitary oaks there is a green track between a fence and a hedge: follow this over a rise and note the church ahead. Fork right where the track splits and continue to meet a lane. Turn left and then right by the **Church of St Mary, Staunton on Wye**. Visit the church, then return to the path along the church boundary. At its end take the less obvious path on the left-hand side of the hedge. Go through a gap into the next field, which may be cropped, and take a middle course, then bear slightly right, then left to find a stile hidden stile in the trees and hedges ahead. Go over and bear left towards an oak, then go around the left perimeter to find a gap into the next field. Follow a track to a stile in a hedge and go over on to a lane. Opposite there is a bridleway. Do not take this: instead, turn right and follow the lane to the A438 and the Portway Inn. Cross, with care, and take the 'No Through Road' opposite, signed Monnington on Wye. After about 300 yards there is a green gate on the left. Go through into an orchard. Follow the left edge and pass a clump of tall poplars, left, to reach a hard-core track. At a corner by an ash tree turn left for 100 yards to reach a boundary hedge: turn right, and where trees form a barrier in front, turn right again and cross a bridge by willow trees. Now head south across the orchard to its far perimeter, then turn right to reach a small gap and a waymarked path on the left. Follow this to **St Mary's Church at Monnington on Wye**. Exit by a doddery lych gate and take the leafy avenue by the large residence to the left. Take the lane, left, and swing right. A long avenue of pine and yew lies ahead. Where the lane bends left, go through the gate ahead and follow a grassy path to a green gate. Take the thinner path beyond going through woods and ascending to a viewpoint overlooking the River Wye. Now, either follow the track down to a lane and turn right back into Staunton (crossing the main road once), or look very carefully in the wood near the viewpoint for a thin track going sharp right. Thread through the trees and cross a field along its left edge. Go through a gap and over a small ditch to reach a stile in the corner of the next field, by a broad oak. Cross the field beyond aiming the corner of a small wood. Just left of a fence is a corrugated plank crossing the stream: follow the nearest hedgerow aiming for the white gable end of a cottage ahead. Turn left at the field top to find a stile on to the main A438. Turn right, with care, passing the cottage to find a right of way. Follow this for 100 yards to reach a lane back to Staunton.

POINTS OF INTEREST:

St Mary's Church, Staunton on Wye - The earliest vicar mentioned here is William Picard in 1220. The font is 700 years old and the tower is 13th century with a medieval timbered roof.

St Mary's Church, Monnington on Wye - The church was built in 1679, though the tower, in perpendicular style, is older. The church has remained virtually unaltered since construction.

REFRESHMENTS:

The New Inn, Staunton on Wye.
The Portway Inn, on the route.

Walk 38 SHELSLEY BEAUCHAMP 5½m (9km)

Maps: OS sheets Landranger 138; Pathfinder 973.

Three fine churches linked by valley and hillside.

Start: At 731629, Shelsley Beauchamp Church.

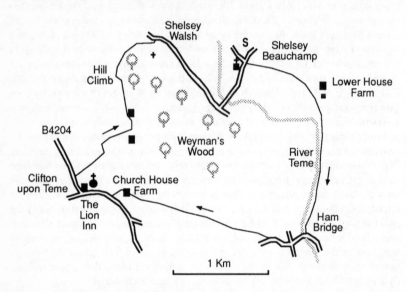

From **All Saints' Church** take a metalled lane opposite on the corner, passing a modern brick bungalow, left, and reaching a farm building housing machinery. Go past an apple orchard and keep to the right of a hedge after the hard-core track becomes dirt. The track flanks lower fields and crosses a small brook. Keep faith when it almost disappears, as it reappears at the edge of a wood. Ascend slightly to reach a gate. Go through and bear right on a wider, obvious track which runs into a field. Keep near the right edge and cross logs over a small brook to gain the next field. The River Teme is concealed behind thickets to the right as this narrower field is followed on its right edge. Pass some numbered fishing posts and go through a rusty iron gate into the next field. Yet another gate and riverside walking leads eventually to Ham Bridge. Cross this, over the River Teme, and take the B4204 westwards. Walk past a minor road, right, and a track, left, for 250 yards to reach a path on the right into wood. Follow this to an iron gate into a field. Climb steeply up and trend rightwards to reach a wooden gate in a corner. Go through into the wood and climb up to reach a field. Follow a wire fence along the right edge of the wood. The track is more obvious now, and slowly climbs through green pasture. Pause for breath and to admire the lovely view of the Teme Valley hills behind. Stay with the hedgerow and trees past a small wood, right, beyond which the track levels out. Pass an old farm with a partially half-timbered facade and tall chimneys, on the right behind some barns, then turn right along the B4204 into the pretty village of Clifton upon Teme. Here, the Lion Inn now beckons the unrefreshed.

Leave the inn to the right and admire **St Kenelm's Church** and the village church green, the latter flanked by black and white half-timbered cottages. On another, smaller green is the black village pump. Follow the string of cottages through the village until a gap is seen by a red brick cottage bearing a yellow sign 'FP, 17 ft.' Turn right up this path going over a stile into a field and walk to a wooden gate with the sign 'Lambs, shut gate please'. Turn left, then immediately right and, after 100 yards, go through a tunnel in the hedge. Cross the middle of the field beyond, with Woodbury Hill straight ahead and the clock tower of Abberley Hall visible. Where the path appears to run out at a hedge, look carefully for a hole in the hedge and duck underneath to reach a stile with a sandstone block on its far side. Go straight down the field beyond and through a wooden gate to reach a track, with a barn to the left. Turn left. By the barn the track becomes metalled to form the Shelsley Hill Climb. Descend this and take the first right turn to the **St Andrew's Church, Shelsley Walsh**. Leave the church to find a minor road. Go right and follow the road back to New Mill Bridge crossing this to return to the start.

POINTS OF INTEREST:

All Saints' Church, Shelsley Beauchamp – The church is 19th century with an older sandstone tower.

St Kenelm's Church, Clifton on Teme – Built around 1200, though the south aisle dates from 1325 and the church was much restored in 1843. Eight, mainly Midlands churches, bear the name of this Saxon child king murdered at 7 years of age.

St Andrew's Church, Shelsley Walsh – The church is Norman with a beautiful screen. The adjacent house was owned by Sir Richard Walsh High Sheriff of Worcester, who was involved in the capture of the Gunpowder Plotters.

REFRESHMENTS:

The Lion Inn, Clifton on Teme.

Walk 39   **UPTON ON SEVERN**   5$\frac{1}{2}$m (9km)

Maps: OS Sheets Landranger 150; Pathfinder 1042.
A generally low-lying but varied walk.
Start: At 853405, in Upton on Severn.

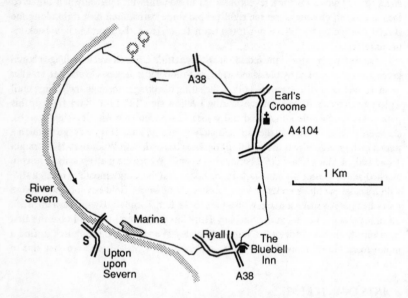

Park in the town and cross the main bridge over the River Severn (the A4104). Just beyond the end of the bridge, dip down right to locate the white rendered 'Bridge End House'. Go between this and 'Bridge End Cottage' on a metalled way, passing a public footpath sign for Ryall. Soon, on the left, note the attractive marina and cross the wooden bridge where the marina is accessed from the River Severn. Go pleasantly along a pleasant green avenue of trees and then go through a wooden gate into a riverside meadow. Eventually you will reach a gap with a thicket on the left: bear away from the river and zig-zag round by some bungalows. Go through a gate and turn left on to an estate road, following it to a T-junction. Turn right through Ryall and cross the main A38, with the Bluebell Inn opposite, to reach The Grove. Pass to the left of the Horse and Groom Inn and turn right into Garden Lane. This cul-de-sac has a walkway on its left: take this and, in a few yards, go right keeping a hedgerow and a ditch on the right. Cross a wooden bridge and follow the edge of a wood for 100 yards before striking left over a field and continuing towards the brow of a hill, leaving a lonely cottage off to the right. Go over a stile and walk over the brow - it is tedious walking through the long grass. Go over another stile and take an undefined route towards a clump of trees slightly to the right and downhill. Cross the A4104 and note a wooden cross on the opposite corner. Set in stone, this cross is dedicated to 8 local men who died in the Great War.

Follow the lane to Earls Croome to view St Mary's Church. Now continue along the lane, ignoring paths on either side. Just beyond some red brick cottages, turn left at the bungalow at the end of a row of houses. Turn right and follow an alley around to reach a stile on the left. Go over into a field. The walk is now undefined again, so go diagonally left and through a gap in the hedge about 30 yards left of a stout oak tree with some dead branches and by willow trees, to the left. Walk to an iron gate and go through it on to the A38. Turn left and, with great care, cross to reach, after about 60 yards, a signed public footpath by Earls Croome Nursery Garden Centre. Follow this path to the river. At first it follows a leafy glade, but later it is choked with yarrow and nettles in late spring. Go along the edge of a field to reach a gap in a hedge. Go through this and an iron gate, and then turn right for a few yards to meet the river. Turn left and walk the long river path, noting Hanley Castle over the water. Upton on Severn can be seen way ahead: eventually the path reaches some steps which can be used to reach a flimsy gate on to the road bridge. Turn right to return to the start in **Upton on Severn**.

POINTS OF INTEREST:
Upton on Severn - Of particular interest to walkers will be the Map Shop', 15, High Street, though the former church, with its baroque tower, is also worthy of note.

REFRESHMENTS:
There are numerous possibilities in Upton on Severn.

Walk 40   FECKENHAM AND BARROW HILL   5¹/₂m (9km)

Maps: OS Sheets Landranger 150; Pathfinder 974 and 975.
A scenic village, a low hill, lanes and fields.
Start: At 009614, Feckenham village car park.

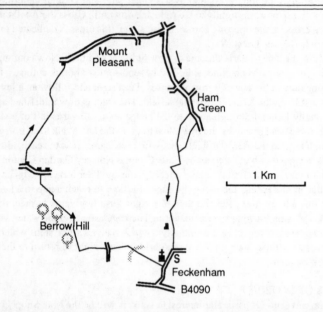

Go out of the car park and turn left along the village street. Turn first left onto the village green with its fine cluster of cottages. Go down the lane on the right, passing the cricket club, to the right. The lane becomes hard-core, then gravel, as it passes through a fine avenue of trees. Go to the right of a former mill, with the race to the right, and cross a bridge over a stream. Now either take the obvious trail, left, to a T-junction and turn right, or go into the trees on a track and go up a short steep gully to the left. Ahead is a stile. The former route requires a turn right along the bridleway to reach the stile, to the left. Go over an uphill for 70 yards to find a waymarked stile and a fine view of Feckenham. Follow a hedge and cross two further stiles before crossing a lane and following the marked bridleway opposite. Dip down near a house with tennis courts, on the left, then go through an iron gate and trend right and uphill to reach a gate. Go through and turn to walk steeply up to the broad ridge of Barrows

Hill. Continue to the trig point and bear left of it to reach a stile in a line of trees about 250 yards away. Go over and down into thickets. This walk section is tricky: look very carefully for a way into the trees on the right or you might finish in thick brambles. A thin path goes through the trees, with a property boundary to the right. At an open field with two black and white houses ahead, bear to the left of them to reach a stile in a corner. Go over and double back around the boundary to reach a white fence and a gate. Turn left on to a drive, and then turn left into a lane.

At the sign and entrance for Upper Berrow Farm, there is a stile on the left: go over into a field. The walk is now undefined, so bear left down towards trees to reach two stiles which are used to cross a small archery range. Follow the right edge of the next field and go through a gap, on the right. Head diagonally right of a deciduous plantation to go through an iron gate and head rightwards across a field, going under pylon lines to locate a gap. Cross a stream over a hard-core-covered culvert and head right of the farm ahead. Skirt the farm on a dirt track, following it to a road. Turn right along the road. Go over at a cross-roads, noting the fine half-timbered house to the right. Go over a brow and walk down to another cross-roads and the Brook Inn at Elcock's Brook.

Turn right on the signed lane to Feckenham and follow it past some fine period cottages. A few hundred yards after passing the left turn at Ham Green, there is a footpath sign on the left. Before this, go over a waymarked stile on the right and walk along a field hedge and fence. Bear right to meet a track coming in from the right at an acute angle. Take a green track to reach a gate/stile. Go over and turn right for 60 yards to reach another stile. Go over and turn left. Leave the fence and hedge to cross a field on a thin, but well seen, path which leads to a stile. Go over, walk along an avenue and go over a stile, and then keep left of a large property to the right. Follow its boundary fence, to your right, to reach and cross a bridge over a stream. Two more stiles lead to a lane into Feckenham. However, take the signed path on the right along an alley and into the churchyard. Exit the yard along a passage between cottages to reach a street and return to the start.

POINTS OF INTEREST:
Feckenham - This picturesque village with many fine cottages. The church, of 13th century Norman origins, is worth a visit.

REFRESHMENTS:
The Brook Inn , Elcock's Brook, Feckenham.
There are also other possibilities in the town.

Walk 41   **ASTLEY**   5¹/₂m (9km)

Maps: OS Sheets Landranger 138; Pathfinder 973 and 974.

A Norman Church and a monastery visited with interesting walking.

Start: At 811677, by the modern houses at The Burf.

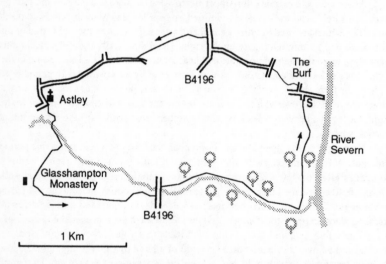

Walk up to the cross-roads made by a bridleway and a lane and turn right into the lane to find a public footpath, to the left, up steps. Continue along a sandy, uphill track rightwards to reach game bird pens. Walk around the perimeter of these, making one 90° turn right. Now where the lane below turns left, get on to it, by Astley Burf Outdoor Centre, and follow it, passing two modern houses, to the left, and Weatherlane Farm, to the right. Turn right on to the B4196 for about 150 yards and then turn left on to a public footpath for Astley Town. Go over a stile, but ignore the next, following, instead, the path as it leads round left and runs beside a copse at the field edge. Ignore another stile to the right and go straight for 150 yards to reach another. Go over this stile and walk along a field to reach a corner stile. Go over, but ignore the next stile, on the left, going straight on through trees to reach the boundary fence of a house to

80

the left. Turn right when a road is reached and walk to a T-junction. A left turn at this junction reveals **St Peter's Church, Astley**.

Near the church there is a hard-core car parking space from which a track descends. Take this, going downhill into a thick wood. In summer this track might be overgrown: keep faith to find a hidden stone bridge to the right. Cross this and a wide track to keep straight on, emerging in a field. The path ascends the middle of the field and soon, on the right, Glasshampton Monastery can be seen. Note the plaque in the facade of the building 'There stood by the cross of Jesus his mother'.

Turn left on a downhill track through fields to reach the B4196. Go left and take the first available turn to the right, by conifers in a driveway. Leave the drive almost immediately to go across two fields below the property which is above and to the left. The way now becomes obvious, going alongside woods, to the left, with a tributary of the River Severn to the right behind the trees. This is a very easy and pleasant section of the walk, passing fenced enclosures to the right and eventually swinging round left, though still following the border of the wood. The peaceful interlude is broken when a corrugated barn is passed, to the right. After a few hundred yards the path leads back to the start of the walk.

POINTS OF INTEREST:

St Peter's Church Astley – The church was founded around 1102 and dedicated in 1289. The modern 20th century porch conceals a fine Norman door. The doorway has been restored. The pillars and main arch are original, as is the font, though it has a 20th century cover. The tower is mostly original. At the west end of the graveyard are tombstones to W V, and his daughter Francis Ridley, Havergal. The former was a minister, while his daughter was a prolific poet, lyricist, and hymn writer in Victorian times. Her prose, revealed in a complete book of her works, is meaningful and moving, reflecting typical Victorian Christian faith.

REFRESHMENTS:

The nearest is *The Hampstall Inn*, signposted by the River Severn.

Walk 42   CHADDESLEY CORBETT AND WOODS   5¹/₂m (9km)

Maps: OS Sheets Landranger 139; Pathfinder 953.

A village, fields and woodland make up this fine walk.

Start: At 892735, Chaddesley Corbett church.

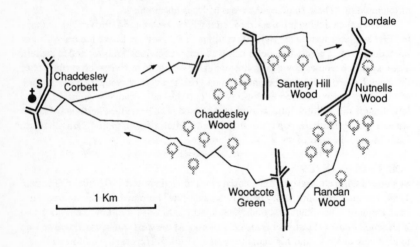

Opposite the spired church in the fine village of Chaddesley Corbett, there is a public footpath: take this into a drive by Spencer House. Soon, the wide drive swings left by some new bungalows and, after another 150 yards, it goes right again by a house sporting a wooden facade. After a further 100 yards or so there is an opening to the field on the left, with two waymarker arrows. Go through and take the thin track across the field's centre, aiming for the cluster of pylons ahead. Go through a gap in the hedge ahead and follow the path across another field. Continue into the next field, heading towards a hedge with some trees. Here there is a stile. Go over and cross a field to reach two successive stiles. At the far side of the next field is an electric fence. Cross where there is a rubber handling tube and go over the stile immediately beyond. Go under what seems to be horse jump to reach another field, turning rightwards to reach a stile on to a farm drive. Cross and go through an iron gate and a small stile.

Now bear left, aiming for a pylon and a stile beneath it. Bear slightly right across a field, then go left, aiming for a dip. Follow the hedge to the left to reach a wood some 150 yards ahead. Go over a stile in the left-hand corner to reach the trees, and go left to leave them. Walk ahead to another stile. Now aim for a pink cottage to reach a lane. Turn left, then right by the far end of the cottage, crossing fields and stiles to reach the border of a wood, where a water main and stile signify the route. Note the National Nature Reserve post with information on **Chaddesley Woods**. Go left over a wooden bridge and then right through thick undergrowth to emerge in a large field. Go past a marshy pool to the right and an orchard to the left. Soon, the path swings left to reach an iron gate and a stile. Go over and turn right on to a road.

The road is followed pleasantly as it threads through woodland. After $^1/_2$ mile turn left at a public footpath sign for Randon Wood. The wood is a lovely interlude, but the route can be muddy hereabouts. Go through a gate to reach a section of fenced path on the edge of a clearing. Pass a farm on the left and swing right, keeping to the major track which leads alongside clearings until it becomes metalled and then reaches a road. Turn right. Just before the junction of Woodcote Green Lane, as the road forks, go over the stile in the hedge, under a telegraph pole.

Go left across a field, go over a broken stile and just before some farm buildings to the left, bear right, noting a yellow waymarker on an iron gate. Now head towards the woods, either by going through an iron gate or a gap in the hedge to the left of it. Go over a stile in the right-hand corner of the field to enter the woods.. Another Nature Reserve sign denotes the correct route: go uphill to a T-junction and turn left on the bridleway flanked by large conifers. A wider bridleway comes in from the right, but as soon as you join this you leave, on a bend, by going straight downhill, an arrow on a tree pointing the way. At the bottom of this descent the track forks. Take the left-hand fork into trees, as waymarked by yellow arrows. The track leads to the edge of the woods where a stile gives access to a field. Chaddesley Corbett is now visible and if the weather is clear, the Clee Hills can be seen beyond. Go over a stile and follow the right edge of a field, beyond which the track is wide and green and soon joins the outward route. Instead of retracing this, go straight ahead on a different track that reaches the village opposite the Swan Inn, a convenient finish for the thirsty!

POINTS OF INTEREST:
Chaddesley Woods - This National Nature Reserve, established in 1973, is an outstanding example of a lowland English oakwood lying mainly on acidic soils.

REFRESHMENTS:
The Swan Inn, Chaddesley Corbett.

Walk 43 FAIRFIELD, DODFORD AND PEPPER WOOD $5^1/_2$m (9km)

Maps: OS Sheets Landranger 139; Pathfinder 953.

Intricate route-finding, varied scenery and terrain underfoot make for interesting walking.

Start: At 946755, the Swan Inn, FairfielÑ

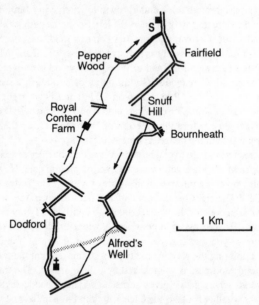

From the Swan Inn, marked PH on the OS and located on the B4091 just north of Fairfield, walk along the ribbon development that is the village, passing Fairfield school and the church, opposite. Turn right into Bournheath Road and very soon maintain direction into Brook Road. Walk to Pepper Wood Cottage, which has stone bollards guarding its driveway and, exactly opposite, find a stile and footpath sign beside a white house. Follow the path to reach another stile and an enclosure with rusty relics scattered about. After another 40 yards, turn right over a stile and pass a corrugated outbuilding and a white cottage, to the left, and follow a metalled drive to reach a lane. Turn left along the lane and just past a large, red-brick detached house, there is, on the opposite side, a holly hedge with a stile beneath it. Go over this into a paddock and follow its left edge to reach another stile in the top corner. Go over to reach a lane. Turn right and follow this pleasant lane downhill to a T-junction. Turn left down steep Niblet's Hill to where it bends left in a deep dell. On the bend there is a footpath sign by a stream: follow this along a delightful secluded valley, wooded on its far bank, to reach a bridge over the stream. Cross and go very steeply (possibly slippery) uphill and left, at first, then trending right through thickets. Go over a stile and cross a narrow green strip into a big field. Go along the left edge to reach a corner where two stiles zig-zag into the next field. Go diagonally left to locate a corrugated outbuilding and a stile on to a lane. Turn right into Dodford. Go past the village school and turn right at the sign for **Dodford church**. Wind around the lane by the very attractive Dodford Farm, seen against a backcloth of far rolling woods. The church is locked these days, but a note in the porch gives instructions on where to obtain the key.

Leave the church by a looping lane which passes Dodford Village Hall and take Church Road, to the left. Walk past the scattered dwellings that make up the village and, at a cross-roads, turn right and rise steadily to reach a T-junction. Go left, and after about 250 yards you will reach a public bridleway on the right, beyond an iron gate. The way is signed for Dordale Road. Hold your nostrils on passing a battery farm behind the hedges to the right. Continue to follow the right-hand hedge past several fields noting, ahead, the trees of Pepper Wood and, beyond, glimpses of the Clent Hills. Pass through the red-bricked Royal Content Farm, and follow its drive to Dordale Road. Opposite is the entrance to **Pepper Wood**. Follow the well-surfaced bridleway through the wood. This rises steadily before emerging at a ruined corrugated barn. Continue along the obvious route, which soon becomes a metalled lane, back to the B4091. Turn left for a few yards to return to the Swan Inn.

POINTS OF INTEREST:

Dodford Church - The church is not of ancient origin but does have an unusual porch attachment, and occupies a sylvan setting.

Pepper Wood - The wood, a remnant of the former Feckenham Forest, is maintained by The Woodland Trust. A sign gives information on its natural history. The wood's name may be derived from Pyppa, the father of Penda, a Mercian King of the 7th century.

REFRESHMENTS:

The Swan Inn, at the start.

There are also other possibilities in Fairfield.

Walk 44   **VOWCHURCH COMMON** $5^3/_4$m ($9^1/_4$km)

Maps: OS Sheets Landranger 149; Pathfinder 1039.

A good route if followed carefully.

Start: At 362365, opposite the church at Vowchurch.

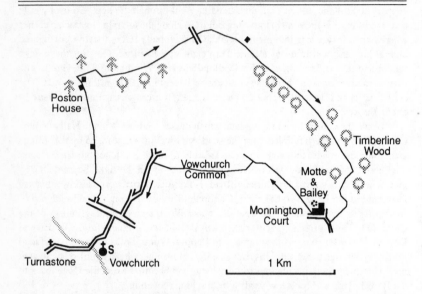

Walk to the T-junction on the B4348 and turn left. Turn right along the first unmetalled drive into a field. Cross the field diagonally left and follow a hedge round, aiming for Cwm Du Cottage ahead. Go over a stile in a fence, pass an old tree stump in undergrowth and reach the building by way of an iron gate. By the edge of a barn, look carefully for a concealed stile, just on the lawn of the property. Go over, pass to the right of a small boggy enclosure and aim directly up the valley to reach a stile and iron gate. Pause here to admire the view back. Now attain the brow of a hill and keep just right of Poston House, going through wooden gates and turning right on the obvious broad track around a tennis court. Head for a fir wood and take the left-hand of two gates into a wood. Swing round right to reach what is almost a dead end. Take the track on the left through the trees and where it forks, keep left along the edge of the wood. Cross the left edge of a small clearing of bracken and carry on along a, possibly muddy, path. A gate gives access to a better track: go under electricity cables on a gravelled section with open spaces to the left, heading towards Garnons Hill. Swing right by an abandoned farm, then go left to follow the edge of a wood. Ignore a stile on the right with blue arrows, continuing to reach a metal gate with a private woodland sign. Walk through a section of younger trees to reach an area of more mature trees. Now descend to reach the junction of many tracks. Turn right, and then left to gain a wide forestry track. Follow this for a few hundred yards, then turn right by a post waymarked with a yellow arrow.

Descend a green track, but after 200 yards or so, look very carefully for a track going into the trees to the left. Just inside the trees there is another yellow arrow indicating a path which contours the slope and then goes down to the right to reach a waymarked gate into an open field. Keep to the hedge on your right until a concealed stile leads to a drive. Turn right to go round the front of **Monnington Court**. Keep the motte and bailey to the right and go through a gap heading towards the white house on the hill ahead. Cut a corner by finding an iron gate in the right corner of the field, and then cross a stone slab over a ditch to gain a wide track. Go past the white cottage to reach a path fork by a shed. Keep left, following the path as it bends rightwards around the slopes of the hill, forming a green lane which eventually emerges on to a steep lane. Turn left and descend to **Vowchurch**, going right and left at the bottom to return to the start.

POINTS OF INTEREST:

Monnington Court – This fine 18th century building is said to be on the site of a former one which housed Owain Glyndwr in the last years of his life.

Vowchurch - Vowchurch is one of two nearby churches, the other being at Turnastone, about $\frac{1}{2}$ mile away. They are said to have been built by rival sisters who could not agree on a site, the names deriving from one sister's vow that she could build her church before her sister could turn a stone on hers. Vowchurch's attractive Norman building is dedicated to many saints and stands, with its timber framed rectory, by an old stone bridge over the River Dore. Inside are impressive timber pillars and a screen carved with the figures of Adam and Eve.

REFRESHMENTS:

There is a hotel in Vowchurch, but nothing more.

Walk 45 BREDON'S NORTON AND BREDON HILL   6m (9½km)

Maps: OS Sheets Landranger 150; Pathfinder 1019 and 1042.
A picturesque village, a stately home and a fine hilltop.
Start: At 931390, in Bredon's Norton.

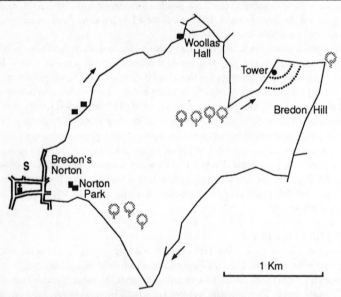

The starts depends on your finding a suitable car parking space, these being in short supply in this fine village. Start by visiting the village church which is situated in its own grounds with no road access. Now walk up the northern of two east-west running lanes in the village to reach a T-junction. Turn left into a 'No Through Road' following it most pleasantly as it bends rightwards, bordered by woodland to the right and with views, to the left, across to the Malvern Hills. After a cattle grid the lane is unmetalled: curve around the buildings of St Catherine's Farm, then pass an isolated cottage, to the right. Kink through the grounds of **Woollas Hall** and, beyond, go over a cattle grid. Continue to reach a stile to the right. Go over and strike diagonally left up the pasture, aiming for three ash trees by a hard-core track. Go through an old iron gate on to the track and follow it to the first sharp bend, left. On this bend, look right for a track going to an iron gate/stile. Beyond, trend diagonally leftwards and uphill, on an undefined route to an iron gate in the top right-hand corner of the field. There, a track is met. Follow this as it contours the hillside. Just opposite is a little gully: a path leads up this into a clump of trees, gained over a contraption of an iron stile. Continue to meet a brown track crossing ahead and turn left along it. Go through a gate and follow a Cotswold stone wall along the edge of a field. The next gate leads directly to the tower capping Bredon Hill. In clear weather the view is extensive: look north towards the Midlands and the Lickey and Clent Hills, and westward towards the Malverns. Just beyond the tower is the **Banbury Stone** in a ditch. Other ditches are formed by the hill fort covering the highest portion of Bredon Hill.

Follow the wall beyond the earthworks to reach a plantation of pines enclosed by a wall. Turn right by the nearside of this wall and a track soon becomes discernible. Go through two gates, still following the wall. Ignore the first track going right and descend gradually to reach another gate. When a sandy track comes in from the left, follow it to reach a walking sign pointing right. Follow this along a hawthorn hedge. Kink round a stone barn on an obvious track, and ignore a path to the right by bearing left. Go through a waymarked gate continuing straight on to where a thin double track leads downhill, by a line of hawthorns, into a coombe. Keep to the line of the hawthorns ascending slightly to reach a fence with a coppice beyond. Now go over a stile into a leafy glade and join another track coming in from the right. Ignore a track going sharp right and go down hill, between hawthorn trees, on the broad track. Just as this way becomes metalled, turn right at a green gate. Walk past clumps of trees on either side to join a track coming from a house far to the left. Where this track deviates, take a path to the left into a field. Go through a waymarked iron gate and then through/over a green gate/stile into a field. Walk along a woodland edge to where another waymarked stile gives access to a rough pasture. Cross to an iron gate. Go through and, at first, head towards a big house (Norton Park). Then, about 150 yards before it, strike left downhill towards electricity posts to reach, by farm sheds, to the right, an iron gate. Go through on to a lane and follow it back to Bredon's Norton.

POINTS OF INTEREST:

Woollas Hall - This elegant 17th century house has some equally interesting outbuildings - the Malthouse and the Coach House.
Banbury Stone - A large outcropping of limestone.

REFRESHMENTS:

Nothing on the route, but available in Bredon village, $1\frac{1}{2}$ miles away.

Walk 46   CROWLE, HUDDINGTON AND HIMBLETON   6m (9¹/₂km)

Maps: OS sheets Landranger 150; Pathfinder 996.

Three worthwhile villages.

Start: At 923563, in the village of Crowle.

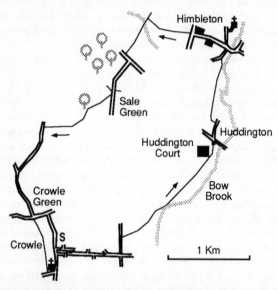

Walk through the attractive village, noting the interesting black and white dwellings. After, perhaps, you have visited the church, locate the school lane and turn right. Bend right by White House Cottages and take the next left turn, going along a straight lane. Turn left at a junction, signed Lower Crowle, and opposite an entrance to a half-timbered, red-brick barn, turn right through a signed gate. Bear slightly left across a field and go over a stile in a fence. Walk to the far corner of the next field there is a stile by a red-brick barn. Circuit this building and keep about 60 yards left of a wood to find a stile in a hedge. Go over this and a bridge across a stream. Follow the stream at first, but where it goes off to the right you will find a stile in a corner. Go over and follow a field edge to reach an iron gate. Kink right and left along the next field, where there is no defined path, to reach a stile beyond a little ditch about 70 yards left of the field's left corner. Go over and cross the middle of a pasture, aiming for the black and white church tower ahead. A stile leads to a farm yard and buildings. Kink right and left through the yard to reach an iron gate, beyond which the beautiful **Huddington Court** is seen to the left, beyond its white gates.

Walk to a cross-roads and go straight over, continuing past two fine period buildings. Go into a field and take the obvious path to the right. Go along the field edge and cross a stile and a plank over a ditch. Walk along the next field and cross two bridges over a stream to reach a stile. Keep to the right edge of the next field to reach a stile in the corner. Cross a paddock and two further stiles to reach a lane. Turn right and then trend left by another period dwelling to reach a T-junction. Turn left. It is possible to visit Himbleton church, but this adds about $1/2$ mile to the walk. The route continues by walking to another T-junction, passing the Galton Arms. Go through an iron gate on to a double track between fields. The track is pleasant at first, but becomes choked with yarrow and nettles. Fortunately, it is possible to walk in the field on the left to reach a gap and an iron gate, to the right. Now turn 180° to see a stile in a hedge and trees. Go over this waymarked stile and a wooden bridge into the next field. Aim for a red brick-house ahead beneath woods to reach a stile and hedge. The path beyond forks: keep right to reach an iron gate and waymarked post. Go left, and then right on to a lane signed for Sale Green and Crowle. Note Trenchwood Nature Reserve, to the right, go past the village telephone box and take the second turning right beyond it. This leads into a drive by houses. Find a gap in a hedge and a stile to the left. Go over and follow the field edge by the wood to the right. Go over a stile in a hedge, turn right, then left along the hedge of the next field and aim for a barn with a red roof. When you meet a vehicular way coming from the barn, turn left. The way becomes metalled and meets a lane: turn left and walk to the T-junction at Crowle Green. Go left of the Old Chequers Inn on a public footpath which gives a view of Crowle church. Follow the path to the church to complete the walk.

POINTS OF INTEREST:

Huddington Manor – Late 14th century with super chimneys, moat, dove cote and gardens. Robert Winter, and Gunpowder Plot members were caught escaping from this place.

REFRESHMENTS:

The Old Chequers, Crowle Green.
The Galton Arms, Himbleton.

Walk 47 THE COMBERTONS AND ELMLEY CASTLE 6m (9$\frac{1}{2}$km)
Maps: OS Sheets Landranger 150; Pathfinder 1019.

A satisfying walk linking four villages and an attractive hill with excellent views.

Start: At 956423, a phone box in Great Comberton.

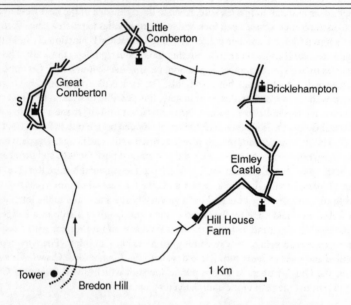

Walk northwards to a fork in the road, just beyond a bend. Take the right fork to reach a signed path after 100 yards. Go into a field and follow overhead cables to reach a bridge over a ditch. Go left, then right, around the edge of a field to regain the line of cables. Cross a plank over a ditch and follow the line of the cables on an indistinct path. Cross another bridge into a pasture. Bear right to the top right-hand corner and go over a stile into a narrow alley through houses. Turn right into Little Comberton. Take Manor Lane, right, and pass two delectable thatched, half-timbered buildings, Meadow and Tudor Cottages. Go round to **St Peter's Church**. On leaving, turn left out of Manor Lane and, after 50 yards, go right over a stile by a sign for Bricklehampton. Cross a field and go through a gate into another, following its edge to reach a stile in a hedge. Go over into to another field. Just before a corner, kink left and go right over a stile. About 50 yards away, around a right angle, there is a stile between a tree and hedgerow: go over and cross tiny brick bridge over a stream. Go diagonally right across a pasture, going under wooden pylons towards a solitary tree and a stile. Go over and aim for Bricklehampton church tower, more like a spire. Go round the last field into a lane. Turn right to pass St Michael's and All Angels Church. Where the road bends, go left, then right on a signed path through vegetable crops that leads to a lane. Follow the lane into Elmley Castle, where either of the villages two inns make a good refreshment stop and the **Church of St Mary the Virgin** is worth visiting.

Go back to the lane and find thatched Bridge Cottage and, beyond, the intriguing Old Police Cottage. Take the path to the left which cuts a corner to approach two further thatched cottages across a field. Go leftwards along a lane, passing more thatched cottages, from the last of which there is a bridleway continuation. Climb to enter open land and keep to a twin track going uphill to reach a clearing where there are several signs. Go left by some firs, then climb diagonally right away from these to reach a boundary fence and a wood with a gate stating 'Wildlife and Countryside Act 1980'. At this T-junction, turn right, and after a few yards the brown track gives way to green grass. Leave the wood and strike right over the open hillside. A distinct scarp with hawthorns is passed to the right. The hill then levels out, offering fine views over the Combertons. Pass a pine plantation within a boundary wall and visit the fort on Bredon Hill before going over a stone stile to return to the wall. Now zig-zag down to gain a central line down the valley, with a wood far away to the right. A fence splits this valley: cross it using two stiles and two gates. Go diagonally right downhill to pick up an obvious bridleway which leads to a farmyard. Go through this to a lane to and head towards the church in Great Comberton. A kissing gate gives access to the church. No walk along the lane back into the village.

POINTS OF INTEREST:
St Peter's Church, Little Comberton – The church is 12th-century, but was restored in 1885-86. The north door is Norman.
St Mary the Virgin Church, Elmley Castle – The church is Norman, but has two 16th-century sundials.

REFRESHMENTS:
The Old Mill Inn, Elmley Castle.
The Elizabeth, Queen of England, Elmley Castle.

Walk 48   **BRITISH CAMP AND EASTNOR PARK**   6m (9¹/₂km)

Maps: OS Sheets Landranger 150; Pathfinder 1041.

Open hills, parkland and woods characterise this walk.

Start: At 763404, the car park at British Camp.

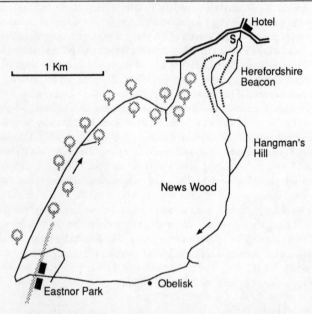

Walk up the path by the stone plaque explaining the **British Camp**, erected by the
Malvern Hills Conservators. Now zig-zag steeply upwards, with excellent views of
the Malvern Hills to the north, and walk through the various troughs of the hillfort
before reaching the flat summit, from where there are fine 360° views. Notable are
Bredon Hill, the Cotswolds, May Hill, Herefordshire's rolling countryside and the
Black Mountains. Continue along the ridge, then make a leftwards descent and swing
right to pass by Clutter Cave, a hole in an outcrop of Malvern granite, man-made, but
with no known history. Skirt through trees on the edge of the wood to the right,
ignoring all tracks to the left, and proceeding to a point where stones and boulders
outcrop on the ridge. The first good view of the **obelisk** in Eastnor Park, to the right,
is from here. Note, too, down below and to the left, the broad green of Castlemorton

94

Common. Just over this top on the descent, look for a thin track running into a much more distinct track, to the right. Follow this into woodland and passing an iron gate on the right. At the second iron gate on the right there are the remnants of a stile: go over this on to a track which leads to a cottage with a gate which has a sign, 'All dogs must be on leads'. Go through this into Eastnor Park and branch leftwards to find a major track leading to the obelisk. It is also worthwhile making a diversion left to climb Midsummer Hill before retracing the steps to the main track to the obelisk.

Parallel tracks now lead on into Eastnor Park before descending by oaks on the right. If you are lucky you may catch sight of the relatively tame deer in the parkland. Carry on down with a view, left, of Eastnor Castle. Keep about 200 yards right of twin lakes, although the right of way is shown running over a strip of land between them. Cross a stream and climb up a track that becomes metalled and reaches a gatehouse. To the left here you will locate a private road sign by a cattle grid on the right. Follow this road, which is called the Ridgeway, through a strip of trees which block views outward, but are well-frequented by many varieties of birds. Note the right-hand track to Netherton Farm, carrying on beyond this to loop right. Where the track splits, take the left-hand fork and climb slightly to pass another gate house close to the main road (A4104). Turn right and, with great care, walk back to the car park.

POINTS OF INTEREST:
British Camp - This Iron Age hillfort is one of the finest earthworks in Britain. It was constructed around the 2nd Century BC, but was enlarged and altered before the Roman Conquest.

Obelisk - The obelisk was erected to the memory of John, Lord Somers, Baron of Evesham and High Chancellor of England, by his eldest son in 1812.

REFRESHMENTS:
At most times there is a Snack Bar opposite the car park.

Walk 49   DORSTONE AND ARTHUR'S STONE   6m (9¹/₂km)

Maps: OS Sheets Landranger 148; Pathfinder 1016.

A well-positioned hilltop and a Neolithic Chamber make this walk a must.

Start: At 313417, the centre of Dorstone village.

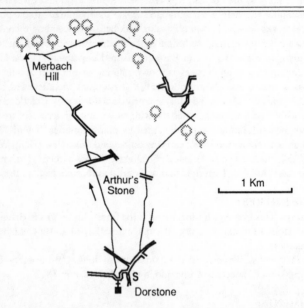

Take the 'No Through Road' which crosses a watercourse and leads to **St Faith's Church**. The path round the churchyard leads to the B4348: cross and go through a gate into a playing field. Go over a stile in the fence ahead and cross a meadow to a footbridge over a stream. Cross this and an old railway line, and go diagonally left to reach another stile. Cross a track beyond and use steps to reach a dilapidated stile in an overgrown hedge. Bear left over the field beyond to reach a lane in the corner. Go left to a farmhouse and turn right on an obvious track. Follow the track to a lane and turn right. Now either go left at the first drive, turning rightwards through fields before a stone house set in trees, to reach a lane, or (longer but simpler) take the lane to the next metalled junction and turn left. Where the lane bends sharp right by a house, go through the gate ahead on to the open hill. Follow a hedge at first, then bear right towards two prominent hawthorns, beyond which there is a gate in a fence-cum-hedge. From the trig. point summit of Merbach Hill, just a few yards beyond, there are outstanding views over the Wye Valley, Hergest Ridge and the Radnor Forest to the north, Hay Bluff and the long edge of the Black Mountains rise above the foothills spreading out of Golden Valley, to the south-west.

Go a little way north of the trig point and take either of two or three thin paths which, after 50 yards, descend steeply to a lateral bridleway. Turn right on this, going straight on beyond a 'Wye Valley Walk' marker post. Where the path appears to bend right, go through the iron gate ahead into a field. Cross this and the field beyond to reach a stile. Go over to reach the edge of a wood and a black barn. Beyond the barn the track descends, curving rightwards to reach Wolla Farm. The track now continues through a plantation and a pasture. When further buildings are encountered, ignore anything to the right to meet a curving lane. Snake round this, ignoring a drive to the right and descend to a signpost for 'Fine Street'. Follow this metalled lane, but where it swings left by a cottage, take a track on the right to reach a stile, also on the right, after only 6 yards. Plod up the hill, go over another stile and along the edge of a wood. Turn left at a stile at the top of the wood and after 150 yards go through an iron gate up right in the fence/hedge. Be careful now: a rightwards circuit reaches another gate. Cross the field beyond to reach a green gate about 100 yards from a farm on the left. Cross the brow of a hill to another gate and follow the left edge of the next field to reach a gate which brings you to a lane, with **Arthur's Stone** directly opposite.

Behind the stone a sign gives the direction for a leftwards descent across a field. Further gates and fields lead to a choice of gates. Take the right-hand one. There are greenhouses down the hill as you walk with a hedgerow on your left. Continue to reach a newish house, and go down a lane to meet the B4348. Follow this back to the church and retrace your steps back into Dorstone.

POINTS OF INTEREST:

St Faith's Church, Dorstone – The church is linked with Richard de Brito, one of the knights who murdered Thomas à Becket in 1170, though it is more likely that a nephew of his, John de Brito, built the church in 1256.

Arthur's Stone - Despite the name this is actually a Neolithic multi-tombed burial chamber dating from between 3700 and 2700 BC. It is the only Neolithic burial chamber in Herefordshire.

REFRESHMENTS:

The Pandy Inn, Dorstone.

There is also a general store in Dorstone.

97

Walk 50   YARPOLE AND CROFT AMBREY   6m (9½km)

Maps: OS Sheets Landranger 148; Pathfinder 972.

Excellent walking country, a picturesque village and a hillfort.
Start: At 471648, in Yarpole village.

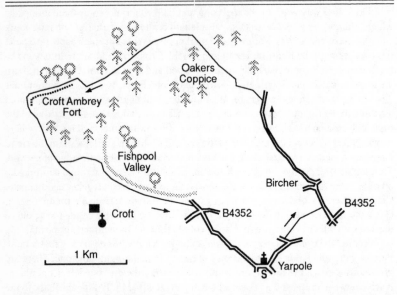

The centre of Yarpole has a tea shop on a corner next to St Leonard's Church. Go left up the lane by the tea shop. Opposite the half-timbered 'Pound House', turn very briefly left and find a gate (almost hidden) into a field by a small brick barn. Follow a distinctive path, at first, then keep to the right of barbed wire enclosures and trend across the pasture to reach a step stile to the right of farm buildings. Go over on to a lane. Turn left and note a four gabled dovecote before turning right at the sign for Leys Lane. This is hedgerowed for ³/₄ mile until it opens out, by two dwellings, on to Bircher Common. Go left and uphill by the cattle grid. Take the second turn right noting Titterstone Clee (with white mushroom!) straight ahead. After 20 yards, turn left by a small beech. Now ignore any turnings from this grassy path, following it to a prominent oak. Turn right to go between trees. Go over at a cross-roads, staying with the brown track as it bears left to reach open pasture. Aim for a group of firs just over the hill ahead (not those to the right). Go left along the edge of a plantation to enter Croft Wood by a sign with its name. Ignore tracks, to the left, following the main track until it bends left. There, go right up a green ride and through a gate. Turn left and walk to the edge of the hill of Lienthall Common from where there are good views over a deep valley, only marred by an open quarry. From here, on clear days, the Arans are visible. More usually, the Radnor Forest, the Black Mountains and Brecon Beacons are seen.

Continue to the **hillfort of Croft Ambrey**, the best part of which is covered by a group of pines. Go down left to reach a gate with sign 'Croft Castle straight on'. To the left of this is a stile: go over on to a path which gives access to more of the earthworks. Go through a gate on to a good track and follow it through woods. As you begin to descend, look left for a gate set back in the trees, beyond which you can glimpse a pink house. Purist walkers can take this, bearing right, downhill past the house, following blue waymarkers through rich woodland to reach the Fishpool Valley, a series of ponds designated as an SSSI. Historians or architects can go straight down across open parkland to Croft Castle (See Note to Walk 51) and the 14th-century Church of St Michael. Note the fine 17th-century bell turret. The wooded section passes a stone hut and eventually joins a metalled lane descending from the castle. Continue to reach a lane and go right by a gate house. Now cross the B4362 into a lane that leads back to **Yarpole**.

POINTS OF INTEREST:

Yarpole – The church of St Leonard has a detached tower above a weather-boarded bell-stage, a most attractive feature. Inside there is a feast of impressive timbers. Opposite the tea shop is a house with a mediaeval gate house in its garden. It is known as the 'Bakehouse' but has also been the village gaol!

Croft Ambrey Hillfort – The name relates to Ambrosius, a Romano-British leader. The fort sits at about 1000 feet and excavations suggest it dates from 550 BC. Traces of up to 300 huts have been found, but the Romans apparently burnt the settlement.

REFRESHMENTS:

The Bull Inn, Yarpole.
The Tea House close to the start is also excellent.

Walk 51 LUCTON, CROFT CASTLE AND YATTON 6m (9¹/₂km)

Maps: OS Sheets Landranger 149; Pathfinder 972.

A recommended additional walk to this picturesque area.

Start: At 437642, in Lucton.

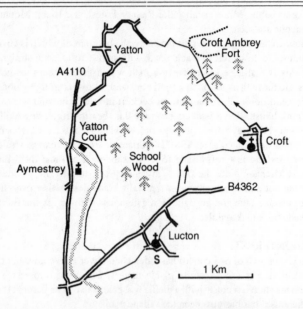

From the old barns in the village go east and turn first left by the timbered Old Forge House. The village church retains its timbered spire and gravestones along the outer edge of the wall, but it is now a private house called 'Old St Peter's Church'. Opposite it, take the signed footpath into a field. Bear right towards a line of ash trees and an old green shack. Go over a stile to reach the school grounds and go right, then left to exit on to a lane. Turn left to reach a T-junction. Turn right along the B4362. About 10 yards beyond the last house on the left, take a signed track through a gate on the left. Across the field to the right is the Spanish Chestnut Avenue. This is the right of way, but is currently fenced off due to fungal disease. Therefore, go over a stile in the top right corner, and another immediately on the right. Follow the avenue's fence and where this ends, join a track (coming from the right), maintaining direction. Where this track bends left, go straight on, through a gate, to a field in front of **Croft Castle**

100

and the adjacent chapel of St Michael. Cross to a gate on to the road through the estate. Turn left, following the road around the backs of some buildings to reach a signed path, heading rightwards towards Croft Ambrey hillfort. Climb to the tree line and go over at a cross-ways to enter Croft Wood. Go over at a second cross-roads and descend slightly to a gate into the hillfort. Contour the base of the fort, then veer left, passing a small isolated rowan tree to reach a clump of prominent pines.

Now swing left sharply and go steeply downhill to reach a building by an avenue of hedges. Pass a detached house and buildings, left, to reach a lane coming in from the right. Go past Yatton Marsh Cottage, then bear left opposite walking signs to reach a postbox in a hedge. Turn left along a narrow lane, passing a rustic timbered building, right. Bear right at a junction, passing a red-brick detached house to reach a right-hand bend. On its left is a path going around a perimeter fence: follow this, threading a way through an old quarry to reach the A4110. Turn left, with care, as far as a signed path to the left, by a gatehouse. The path skirts Yatton Court, seen to the right. Cross a little stream and trend right, going over a stile and crossing to the top right-hand corner of the next field, by some fir trees, where there is a hidden stile. Go over and turn right through pleasant woodland with the River Lugg close at hand to the right. Finally, bear left to a gate. Go through, leaving the wood, and following a field edge past an outbuilding and a bungalow to reach the B4362. Here, either turn left back to Lucton, or (and better) turn right to reach **Mortimers Cross Mill** on the right. Opposite the mill there is a footpath in the hedgerow: go over a stile, cross a field on a convenient path and follow field edges all the way back into Lucton.

POINTS OF INTEREST:

Croft Castle - Started in the 14th century, though all but the four corner towers dates from the 18th century. Owned by the Croft family from the Conquest until 1746. Now owned by the National Trust. The Spanish Chestnut Avenue is the only one of its kind in the country.

Mortimers Cross Mill – This 18th-century water mill is still in use. It is open Thursday, Sunday and bank holiday afternoons from April to September.

REFRESHMENTS:

The Bull Inn, Yarpole.

Walk 52 **THE CLENT HILLS** 6m (9$\frac{1}{2}$km)

Maps: OS Sheets Landranger 139; Pathfinder 953.

Excellent hills with something of a Welsh Marches flavour.

Start: At 943803, Walton Hill car park.

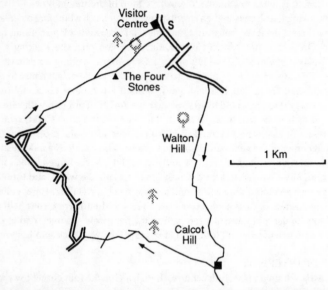

From the car park, locate the waymarked North Worcestershire Path and follow it eastwards on a circuitous route between trees. Round the base of Walton Hill and zig-zag to its broad ridge which is followed to the summit and trig point. An alternative is to climb the steep staircase direct to the ridge. The hill is at 1035 feet (315 metres) and is the second highest point in Worcestershire, ouside of the Malverns. Its position offers superb views - on a clear day ten counties can be seen. To the left, the breccia sandstone hills roll away towards the Lickeys. Ahead, the Malverns and the Black Mountains can be seen. There are also fine views of Birmingham, and the Black Country beyond, and of Adams Hill, decked with its distinctive beeches.

From the summit, trend slightly left and follow a good path, with waymarker posts, to reach a cottage. Go left on a track, then bear right over two short-spaced stiles. Now follow a delightful path bounded, to the right, by hedgerows and offering open views to the left. Stunted hawthorn, ash trees of elegant proportions and Turkey Oak deck the hillside and, to the far left, is a glimpse of Birmingham with its Post Office Tower, a well-known landmark. Two benches, erected by the Wednesday Wanderers Rambling Club and both giving fine views, are passed on the way to a stile by a row of ash trees with a prominent white cottage well below. Go over and keep ahead for 30 yards to reach a stile in a hawthorn hedge. Go over and turn right to circuit the boundary of Calcot Hill Farm. Go over a stile and turn right along a descending brown track. Dip down between trees to reach a potentially muddy section at the end of a plantation. Beyond, level walking along a track heads towards Walton Farm. Cross over a lane into a field and follow the left boundary fence to reach a stile in the corner. Go over on to a lane and turn right. Follow the lane, passing Clent Hall, to the right. The lane bends round to reach St Leonard's Church, Clent and a cross-roads. Cross and follow a path by a stream. Pass an old school building (now a private house) and a nursing home, to the right, beyond which a narrow pavement under holly hedges reaches Mount Lane, also to the right. Follow this past the Mount Hotel and some houses and then climb past cottages to reach the Hill Tavern and, opposite, a café.

Climb on to the open hillside (National Trust) and make for the skyline. The path levels out after the initial pull, but beyond a clump of pines the gradient increases again for a steady climb to the summit, reached after passing an isolated group of sycamores, to the left. On top are the **Four Stones**. To the right of the summit trig point is a toposcope detailing the extensive view which includes features as far away as the Berwyn Mountains in Clwyd. Keep to the wide gravelly track and head over another lump to enter the fine beeches atop Adams Hill. Descend leftwards to reach the Clent Hills Country Park Visitor Centre where information and refreshments are available. At the lane, turn right, and, after 400 yards, turn right. Turn left by High Harcourt Farm, recently acquired by the National Trust, and follow the lane back to the car park and starting point.

POINTS OF INTEREST:

The Four Stones - These are not ancient, but were erected by the Lyttleton family who once lived at Hagley Hall, which can possibly be picked out below and to the left. The nearby castle-like folly is a similar construction.

REFRESHMENTS:

The Hill Tavern, on the route.
The café/snack-bar opposite the Tavern and the Visitor Centre also offer possibilities.

Walk 53   BISHAMPTON AND CHURCH LENCH   6m (9¹/₂km)

Maps: OS Sheets Landranger 150; Pathfinder 996, 1019 and 1020.

Flat at first, then hilly with woods.

Start: At 990517, Bishampton Church.

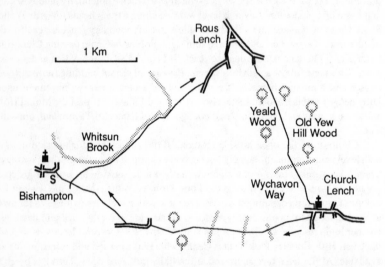

Go eastwards to reach a bridleway on a sharp bend. Follow this for 400 yards, then look carefully for a waymarked post on the left, pointing over a stile. Follow the right edge of the field beyond. After 250 yards, go over a stile in a hedge by trees and follow the left edge of the field beyond to find another stile in a corner under electricity cables. Go past a plantation of willows and poplars on the left and cross two stiles and a footbridge. Now follow a perimeter fence to reach a stile on the left. Cross this and a footbridge. Follow a hedge and trees which enclose a stream and go over a stile and plank, ignoring a footbridge on the left. Just before the elongated corner of the field there is a stile on the right. Go over and go leftwards round trees to another stile. Go over, cross a bridge over a stream, to the left, and go right to a stile in a gap. Go across a field and under electric cables to reach another stile. Cross this and a field to reach a lane. Go left, and left again at a junction to reach Rous Lench. Turn right and take a lane south-east passing **St Peter's Church** and, after several hundred yards, take a gravelled drive going diagonally right. Go past a couple of houses and continue on a green avenue by an orchard. Go over a stile into an open field, with sudden open views towards the Malvern Hills, May Hill and Bredon Hill, and go along the edge of a steep dip in the field to find a stile into a wood. This thick woodland is traversed by the Wychavon Way: bear right by a Way post and leave the wood over a stile. Now follow the woodland boundary, to the left, and cross a footbridge and stream at the bottom. Go immediately left and right, and climb steeply. Round some bramble bushes and go over a stile on the right. Follow the edge of a plantation and go over a stile by a gate.

Ahead now is All Saints' Church, Church Lench, charmingly situated on a hilltop. On the nearest pillar to the inner door is an old sign stating 'Neglect not to give alms'. Take the Evesham Road, signed on a fence by a house opposite the church, and after 100 yards, go right by the white gable end of a cottage whose drive gives a right of way. Follow a fence, dipping downhill to cross a stile into an open field. Cross a bridge over a ditch in the bottom right corner of the next field and maintain the line to reach a gate. Go through, cross a bridge and the next field to reach a stile. Go over and climb up, keeping about 70 yards away from the boundary hedge on the left to reach a concealed stile in the tree and hedge line ahead. Go over and descend awkwardly through a thicket to emerge onto a golf course. Follow the right edge and then go to the right of a hedge and follow it to reach a lane on a bend. Turn left, then bear right immediately towards power cables to reach a bridleway, just before them, to the right. Follow the way back into **Bishampton**.

POINTS OF INTEREST:
St Peter's Church, Rous Lench - The church is Norman with a 12th century arcade. Tombs and tablets of the Rous family (who gave the village its name) can be seen in the Rous Chapel.
Bishampton - The village church here, St James', is also Norman, the earliest recorded vicar being Thomas de Pippard in 1200.

REFRESHMENTS:
The Dolphin Inn, Bishampton.

Walk 54 HAWFORD DOVECOTE AND SALWARPE 6m (9½km)

Maps: OS Sheets Landranger 150; Pathfinder 974.

An attractive canal side in a pocket of secluded countryside.

Start: At 846607, Hawford Dovecote.

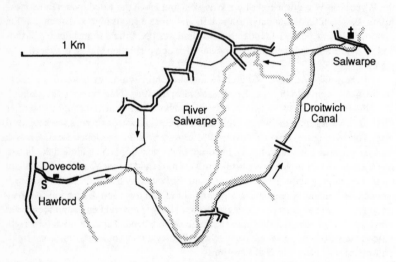

Take the obvious track, by the drive to **Hawford Dovecote**, to Hawford Grange Barn.
Go left over a stile and round a pond to reach a hard-core drive Where it forks, keep
left, going downhill by the edge of a copse. Keep to the fence on the left and go over
a stile at the foot of another copse. Cross a field, keeping power cables to the right,
and go over a stile in a hedge. Turn right, cross a bridge over the River Salwarpe and
then another bridge. Go through two gates and double back around a property to
reach a gate. Go through and U-turn to gain a canal towpath at a bridge with a lock
just beyond. The canal's reeds are a haven for wildlife. Proceed in a tranquil setting,
passing a beautiful half-timbered house on the left. At a lane (and bridge), turn left
and immediately right by Lock Cottage (No 1). Follow a lane to the entrance of a tip.
Go into the tip, the only blot on this landscape, to pick up the canal towpath again.
Beyond next bridge, and Lock Cottage (No 2) opposite and an attractive mooring

basin, the towpath is narrower and overgrown in places. Go under the bridge at Salwarpe and continue for another 200 yards to pick up a path which doubles back into the churchyard.

Go out of the churchyard and turn right down a lane to a bend, where there is a stile, to the left. Now follow yellow arrows (on post and stile) to reach steps back on to the towpath. Turn right. On the opposite bank is a long brick wall: just before the end of this, look carefully right for a thin path down to a stile in a thicket. Go over this and two further stiles. After the second, go diagonally right (as waymarked) to cross a bridge over the River Salwarpe. Follow the path beyond to the end of the field. To avoid the nettles, it is better to turn right for a few yards and then left on to a track, passing the true, signed path after some yards. Proceed along the track, passing a newish detached house on the right, to reach a metalled lane.

Turn left to the river bridge and, just before it, turn right over a stile into a field. Turn right and walk around the end of a hedge. Cross diagonally over the field beyond to reach a gap in a hedge. Follow the next hedge on the left to reach a concealed gap in the hedge ahead where there is a plank over a ditch. Cross to reach a lane. Turn left. At a T-junction, with a corner cottage, turn right. On the first bend, it is possible to go right on a system of poor rights of way which become virtually lost. It is better, however, to follow the lane around to a signed bridleway on the left. Take this along a hedge and at the lateral hedge ahead, turn right. The path forks by a hedge: take the left fork, going diagonally left across a field. Turn left along the hedgerow to reach an iron gate, with a stream and ditch on the right. Ignore the first stile in the hedge on the right: just beyond is a second one. Go over on to the outward route and retrace it to the Dovecote.

POINTS OF INTEREST:
Hawford Dovecote - This superb 16th century half-timbered dovecote is now owned by the National Trust. Normal opening hours apply.

REFRESHMENTS:
None on the route, but available in nearby Ombersley or Droitwich.

Walk 55   CLEEVE PRIOR AND CLEEVE HILL   6m (9¹/₂km)
Maps: OS Sheets Landranger 150; Pathfinder 1020.
A pleasant river walk, a scenic village and a small hill/ridge.
Start: At 067471, the Fish and Anchor Inn, on the B4510.

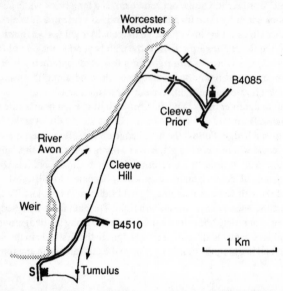

Walk along the road, at the riverside, towards Cleeve Prior and go left through a
caravan park (signed for Cleeve Prior). Beyond the park, keep to the river bank, passing
a weir and some cottages. Eventually you will reach a strip of woodland: ignore a
path to the right, going straight on to join a metalled track. Follow this around to the
right by a life belt holder. Ignore a signposted path to the church and go slightly left
and uphill through woods, trending right by a cottage, to the right. Go straight over at
two cross-roads of paths to reach a T-junction of paths. Go straight over and walk
with a hedge to the right to reach the end of a field, going through a gap to the right.
Keep a hedge on the left in the next field to reach a stile. Go over and turn right to
cross a plank bridge and another stile. In the next field aim slightly left of the church
tower at Cleeve Prior, ahead. Note the old hall to the left and cross a stile by a tree.
Now enter the churchyard through a gap in a hedge.

Leave the **church** through a metal gate between stone buildings and follow a pebbled drive to the Kings Arms Inn. From the inn, turn left on the B4085, following it around a sharp corner. Continue for about 600 yards to reach the next left bend. Just around this corner, Mill Lane goes off to the right: take this, passing through a new housing development. Go over the brow of a hill and then take a bridleway to the left, signed for Littleton. Traverse the tree-lined ridge of Cleeve Hill, from where there are good views, to the right, over the River Avon. After about $1\frac{1}{2}$ miles the way reaches the B4510. Turn right for about 50 yards and then go left on a signed path. Go past an orchard, to the left, and continue over a right of way to reach a tumulus. Virtually at the corner of an enclosed track, turn right and right again immediately to follow a hedgerowed track. Go through fields to regain the B4510 and simply turn right to return to the Fish and Anchor Inn.

POINTS OF INTEREST:
Church - Cleeve Prior church contains the curious grave of Sarah Charlett. She died in 1793, apparently at the age of 309! This is a stonemason's mistake. Having spaced the figures 3 and 9 too far apart, a circular flourish was inserted to fill the gap.

Although not on the route, the nearby Middle Littleton Tithe Barn is worth a visit. The restored 13th-century building is 136 feet long and built of blue lias stone. It is still in use as a farm building, but is in the care of the National Trust.

REFRESHMENTS:
The Fish and Anchor, at the start.
The Kings Arms, Cleeve Prior.

Walk 56 BRIMFIELD AND MIDDLETON ON THE HILL 6m (9½km)
Maps: OS Sheets Landranger 138; Pathfinder 972.
Rolling country, two historic churches and 200 yards of jungle!
Start: At 526678, the Roebuck Inn at Brimfield.

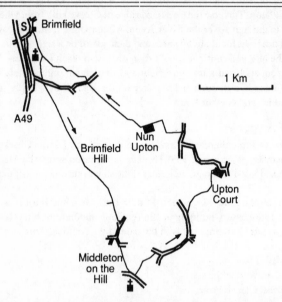

Where white cottages adjoin the inn take a signed lane leftwards. At farm buildings beyond houses, a gate and enclosure lead to another gate with a kissing gate beyond into the churchyard of **St Michael's, Brimfield**. Go through a kissing gate on the opposite side of the churchyard and through an orchard to reach a double stile into a field. Follow the right hedge uphill to reach a stile on to a lane near a half-timbered cottage, left. Cross to the signed stile opposite. Go along the left edge of a field and, just right of the corner, go over a bridge and stile in the trees. Go past a new house (not on the current map) and aim for a stile at the right end of five trees. Descend a rough orchard and cross a bridge over a stream into a field. Keep to the left boundary, going across a plank over a ditch and a stile. Climb Brimfield Hill and keep to the left boundary to reach a stile. Crest the hilltop and keep to the hedge again to reach a stile into a wood. The wood can be very overgrown: plough through to reach a stile on the left end boundary. Normal walking follows: go across a field and a bridge over a ditch, and walk along a hedge. Go through a gap in the hedge and over an overgrown stile on to a lane. Go straight ahead to a T-junction and there bear right on a track. Take the first track left and after 100 yards go through a gate and walk diagonally right across a field.

This little used right of way reaches an awkward fence with a stile (of sorts) behind it. Cross this and the field beyond to reach a gap between large farm buildings. Go through on to a drive and follow it to the **Church of St Mary the Virgin**. Leave by the far gate and cross the drive to a gap in the wall where there are two walkway signs. Follow the left of these towards an isolated tree, beyond which is a plank bridge/ stile over a ditch. Cross the next field to a stile on to a lane. Turn right along the lane and go left at the next junction. Ignore a lane coming in from the right bearing left and dipping down to reach a concealed stile, to the left. Do not go over: instead, take the green track beyond the gate opposite. Go along a hedge and field boundary, going right, then left at the top. Go through a gate and cross a field towards Upton Court, crossing open lawn and a yard, then going left on to a lane. Walk to a T-junction and turn right. Take the next turn left to reach a gate signed Nun Upton. Go through a farm and two gates and bear right into a field. Go just right of some ash trees and downhill to reach a stile in a hedge just left of an isolated house. Cross an orchard garden and a field to reach an a waymarked stile. Head towards barns to reach a waymarked gate. Now trend right through the gated yard of a cottage and go down its drive to a T-junction. Just left of this there is a hidden stile in the hedge: go over and bear left to a double stile in a corner. Go over and continue over further stiles to reach Brimfield church and the route back to the starting inn.

POINTS OF INTEREST:
St Michael's Church, Brimfield - The church was built in about 1100, but has later additions and changes.
St Mary the Virgin Church, Middleton on the Hill - St Mary's has a Norman font, and chancel arch and the nave roof is timber-trussed.

REFRESHMENTS;
The Roebuck Inn, Brimfield.

Walk 57   SHATTERFORD AND UPPER ARLEY   6m (9¹/₂km)

Maps: OS Sheets Landranger 138; Pathfinder 952 and 932.
A walk of great scenic quality, forest and riverside scenery.
Start: At 791812, the Bellman's Cross Inn, Shatterford.

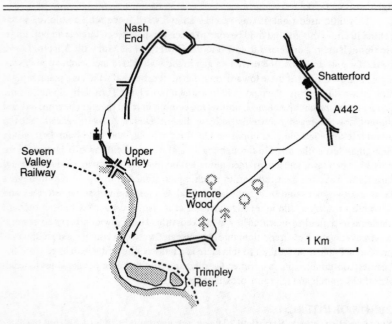

From the inn, walk north-west, with great care, along the A442. Go over a cross-roads and almost as far as the pylons. Go through a gate on the left and keep Titterstone Clee ahead to reach a gap. Go slightly right down a field, keeping left of two modern barns. Cross a step, keep along a fence and go over a stile on the left. Go under cables and descend to a white gate/stile. Go over and through a coppice, crossing a stream by a plank to reach another stile. Hug a wood edge, but where it bends left, go straight on towards a line of trees. Follow a track to a gate and farm buildings. Bear left on the farm drive, with a bungalow to the right. Turn left at a T-junction and follow a lane, swinging right by a farm building. Go left into its yard by an open barn and take the right-hand of two gates. On reaching a coppice, cross a concealed stile on the left and go down a field edge to a reach a house. Note that the OS map shows the path on the south side of the stream. It is possible to go that way to reach the same point. Go right along the track to reach a T-junction. Turn right for about 100 yards to reach a signed path and double back through a field with young caged trees. Now head towards Arley Church, continuing on the road through the Arley House Estate. Go left through two stone portals and a gate and go past a turreted tower to reach a gate at the end of the estate. Turn right to visit **St Peter's Church, Upper Arley**. Retrace your steps and descend to the River Severn. On a bend in the lane, take the concrete path to the riverside. At a little stone bridge, the path divides: keep to the river path in a sylvan situation, passing under Victoria Bridge (See Note to Walk 96).

Now either go around the base of Trimpley Reservoir or hike up to, and around, its perimeter. Go left on the concrete road by a lower lake and swing around it. Go over a stile on the left, cross the Severn Valley Railway and go through a gate up into a wood. Take the left fork on the track in the wood, with conifers to the left and oaks to the right, to gain Eyemore Wood picnic area and car park. Turn right out of the site and follow the road uphill. There are now two options: either take a broad ride to the left, swinging right and then turning left to reach the signed Worcestershire Way, or go uphill and around a bend to reach a gate, to the left, by a lay-by. The track beyond crosses a stream to a Worcestershire Waymarker. The options join: follow the Waymarkers. Go along a ride and ford a stream. Turn left at a T-junction, and immediately right at another T-junction. At the next T-junction, turn left, downhill, noting a shack ahead. Turn right at cross-ways before this and follow Worcestershire Waymarkers, looping round left and dropping down to cross a bridge over a stream. Turn right, upstream, on little steps on the edge of a wood. The track now goes leftwards and under pylon lines. Cross a stile, and climbing uphill through deciduous woodland passing a shed, a gate/gap and a wooden dwelling. A broad driveway leads to a lane: turn left to reach the A442 and the start point.

POINTS OF INTEREST:
St Peter's Church, Upper Arley - There is the effigy and tomb of a Crusader inside this fine Norman church.

REFRESHMENTS:
The Harbour Inn, Upper Arley, on the far side of the river bridge.
The Bellman's Cross Inn, Shatterford.

BLISS GATE AND ROCK 6m (9½km)

Maps: OS Sheets Landranger 138; Pathfinder 952.
Undulating, mainly undefined walking in good scenery.
Start: At 747725, the Bliss Gate Inn.

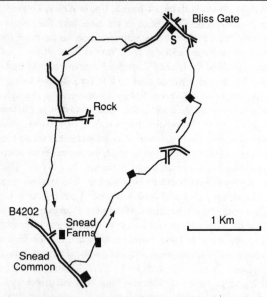

Take the lane signed for Rock Village and Pensax following it down steeply and crossing a stream. About 100 yards further on, turn right on a path which follows the edge of a wooded dell. Go along wood edge into a field and over a step stile into another. Cross a bridge, to the right, over a stream and go diagonally left up a field to a gate in its top right corner. Go through into an orchard and cross to a gate. Go through and follow a tree-lined drive, passing a house, to the left. Just before a white gate on the drive, go left over a stile and head down a field towards Rock village, ahead. Go over a stile, a bridge over a stream, and another stile by a small sewage plant. Cross a field to reach a gate on to a lane and follow it up into the village to reach a T-junction. Turn right into the village to visit the **church.** Turn left on a drive alongside the church, going towards a farm. To the left, in the field, beneath trees, is the ditch of a former moat. A gate, waymarked by a yellow arrow, allows you to go around the farm to reach two gates. Go through the right-hand gate, and a further gate, and then bear right and downhill to cross a bridge over a stream. Walk along the stream to reach a step stile in a fence. Go left and keep a hedge on your left as you climb to a gap. Maintain direction to Upper Snead Farm using a gate to pass its red-brick house. Turn right on to a driveway to reach the B4202 and turn left along it, crossing Snead Common to reach the Bell Inn.

Retrace your steps, passing a footpath on the right to reach a metalled lane, also on the right. Follow this down to meet another lane coming in from the left. Now head towards Snead Farm, a fine period building. Pass it leftwards on the farm track, following it until it suddenly disappears in a large field. Go round the right perimeter of the field and descend left to the bottom right corner. Splash across the stream and take a central line, uphill, towards cabins, some formed from sections of old lorries, trucks etc. Go round a dwelling from the left and round its opposite elevation to pass another cottage on a green path swinging right over a fallen gate. Immediately, go left over a stile and bear left across a field with fine views, right, of the Abberley Hills. Head towards a black and white building beyond the trees ahead to reach a stile to the left of it. Follow a holly hedge to a stile on to a drive. Turn left and follow it to a lane. Turn right, and take the first signed path to the left. Trend right to reach a stile. Go over and descend, keeping a central line to reach a bridge over a stream at the bottom. Go 30 yards right to reach a stile in a thicket. Go over an aim for a modern house on the hill, just right of which is a stile. Go over, turn left past the house and bear right, keeping a black barn to the left, to reach three other barns. Go between the middle and right ones. Ignore the gate ahead, going through one immediately to the right before it. Go down a field to a stile 100 yards left of its bottom right corner. Go left along a thin path to a stream. Cross wherever is feasible and head towards a beige cottage. Go over a stile and bear right around its inner boundary to reach a drive. Walk along the drive to a lane and follow it upwards, returning to Bliss Gate.

POINTS OF INTEREST:
St Peter and St Paul Church, Rock - The church has the largest Norman arch of its type in Worcestershire.

REFRESHMENTS:
The Bliss Gate Inn, at the start.
The Bell Inn, Snead Common.

Walk 59   ILLEY AND FRANKLEY   6m (9½km)

Maps: OS Sheets Landranger 139; Pathfinder 933.

A delightful walk despite the motorway and suburbia's edge.

Start: At 983817, the Black Horse Inn, Illey.

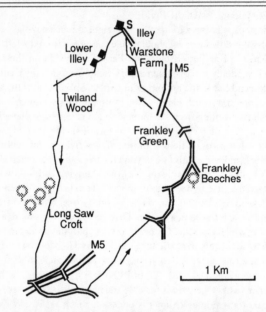

At the far end of the inn car park, take the path signed for Romsley and Waseley. This hard-core drive rises slightly to a crest beyond a hedge where Romsley Hill, Walton Hill and Adams Hill can be seen. To the right of these is the prominent chimney stack of the Bluebird Toffee Works. Descend past houses and Lower Illey Farm, ignoring a track to Frankley, left. Now follow waymarking arrows as you go over a covered brook and bear right by a post marked 'Illey Way'. Cross a stile, with a view of the crest of beeches on top of Adams Hill ahead. Descend into a thicket on wooden steps which cross a brook twice, the second time on a bridge which leads to a stile into a field. At a post showing cross routes, turn left over a stile into a field and make for a wood ahead. To the right is an old railway embankment, a relic of the line that once served the car works at Longbridge. The sylvan way through the wood crosses a stream and climbs a ramp where a yellow arrow waymarker points out a right turn.

Emerge from the wood into a long field. Pass two further waymarker posts, the second giving a kink right, and go straight on up a track between trees. Go slightly right into a field, then kink right and left and, after another 40 yards, cross a waymarked stile. Cross two further stiles to reach a gate where an arrow indicates a right trend. Follow the way uphill to a stile. Go over and turn left on to a road. After about 400 yards look carefully for a signed path concealed in the right hedge. Take this, going over the M5 motorway by footbridge. Turn right into a field, then left into the next one to reach a stile on a tree-lined boundary. A thin copse leads to a lane: turn left, then go left into a property left bounded by a wooden fence. Bear right by the fence. The track dwindles to a thin path through trees, then opens out slightly and rises through thick bushes with the M5 on the left.

When the backs of houses are reached, keep to the obvious path by a lamp-post. Take the higher or lower of two paths across rough ground and cross a bridge with metal rails. Turn right into the field beyond and bear left around its edge to reach a stile. Cross and go right on a green track towards some prominent barns (for conversion) to reach a gap in the hedge by a footpath sign. (The actual right of way goes straight across the field, but it is usually cropped). Go through to the front of the barns and turn right on to a lane. Turn left to reach a 'Give Way' sign. From here the Lickey Hills can be seen, to the far right, and, if it is clear, Meon Hill is also visible. Take the road round towards **Frankley Beeches**, the prominent dome of trees ahead. Turn right into a field and follow its right hedge to reach the trees. Turn left along the road and, after 300 yards, go left, as signed, into a field. Aim for a pylon and go over a stile. Cross a lane into another field and follow a signed path through a thicket and across a field. Go under the M5 by tunnel, go over a stile and cross diagonally right through a field gap to reach Warstone Farm. Follow its drive to reach a lane and the Black Horse Inn.

POINTS OF INTEREST:

Frankley Beeches - A tablet of stone once told of the donation of this land to the National Trust by the Cadbury family, but only the base remains. From the site there are excellent views of the Clent Hills, the Long Mynd, Caer Caradoc, Wenlock Edge, the Wrekin and the Black Country skyline with a glimpse of Cannock Chase. There is also a superb view of Birmingham with the Frankley Reservoirs as foreground.

REFRESHMENTS:
The Black Horse Inn, Illey.

Walk 60　HAY ON WYE AND CUSOP HILL　6m (9¹/₂km)

Maps: OS Sheets Landranger 148; Pathfinder 1016 and 1039.

An elevated open hill, then typical Herefordshire fields and woods.

Start: At 229423, Hay car park.

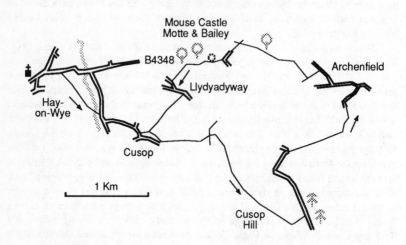

Be prepared to pay and display at Hay! Cross the fields towards Cusop and go over the footbridge across the Dulas Brook to reach the main village street between cottages. Near the Rosedale Bed and Breakfast, turn left on a lane signed for the **Ancient Church of St Mary**. Turn left to reach the church. From the church door a path leads left through a gate into a field. Turn right, as waymarked, towards Cusop Hill. Bear left beyond a gate to go along a tree-lined ditch. Leave this to go straight up a field to reach a stile/gate and then go steeply uphill to reach a lateral track. Loop around this to gain the hill spur. The gradient eases: switch back left and then right to reach the open elevated portion of this fine hill, with views to Hay on Wye and the hills beyond, and to Hay Bluff. Bear left below the crown of the hill to reach a fence stile. Go over and trend slightly right across a huge rough pasture towards a line of trees. Aim at the centre of the line to reach a stile. Go over on to a lane and turn left. Go downhill around one bend and at a second, where the road swings left, go right along a wide track. Go through a gate and over a waymarked stile on the left (a path diversion) and keep just inside a young plantation. From here there are grand views, to the left, over the Wye Valley. Descend through taller trees to reach a waymarked stile. Go over into a field. Head for a gate and waymarked track and go left along it to a farm.

Go through the farmyard and along the drive, then turn left by a corner cottage on to a lane. Turn first right, signed Archenfield, and go down through a dip between buildings. About 100 yards uphill beyond there is a rather concealed stile in the hedge on the left, by a modern barn. Take this and walk beside the barn to reach a waymarked stile. Go over and cross a field to another stile. Go over and turn right along the field edge. A white cottage appears 100 yards to the right: stay with the hedgerow and field edges, briefly walking a track, but soon leaving it to continue along the hedge, heading towards trees. Ignore a gate entering a wood and turn left through another gate to reach a barn/cottage. Pass round this and turn right along its drive, following it through a gate to reach a T-junction. Turn right on a re-directed path (a 1993 alteration). This green path goes between hedges, then goes through a signed gate into 'Woodland Trust' land. Turn left and contour right around a hill. Take a left fork and descend to reach a waymarked stile into a field. Aim for a house (Llydyadyway). Turn left at the lane meeting a drive from the house and, beyond, go uphill to reach a right of way, on the right, which traverses the base of Cusop Hill to arrive at St Mary's Church again. Now retrace your steps to the start point in **Hay on Wye**.

POINTS OF INTEREST:
St Mary's Church, Cusop – The church is Norman and was originally dedicated to St Cewydd, Confessor, a Welsh saint who is the equivalent of the English St Swithin. The chancel arch is early 12th century, the font 13th century.
Hay on Wye - Bibliophiles, at least, will want to visit this charming little village, renowned as the book capital of Britain.

REFRESHMENTS:
None on the walk, but there are numerous choices in Hay on Wye.

Walk 61　**Tardebigge and Worcester Canal**　6m (9½km)

Maps: OS Sheets Landranger 139 and 150; Pathfinder 974.

Countryside flirting with the edge of Bromsgrove and a fine canal walk.

Start: At 997692, St Bartholomew's Church, Tardebigge.

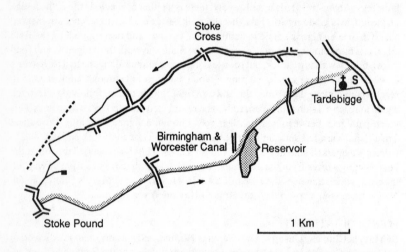

Walk up to the church, with its elegant 135 foot spire, continuing beyond it on a paved path near the church school. Turn right along a hedge, go over a stile and descend towards the canal, with views over Bromsgrove beyond. Go over a stile on to the towpath and walk past a cottage owned by British Waterways, continuing to the first bridge. Scramble up and over this, and the stile beyond, and trend rightwards across a field. Go over a stile and cross a boggy brook in the corner by way of a plank/ bridge. Just to the left is the next stile: go over and walk between hawthorn bushes to reach another plank/bridge. Cross this and the field beyond to reach a gate and a footpath sign. Turn left along a lane, soon passing a white gabled house, and continuing to reach the converted 'Willow Barn' and the adjacent, attractive period house with its mullioned windows and a suspended half-timbered gable on pillars acting as a porch. Although metalled, the lane offers a pleasant walk; continue as far as St Godwall's Road and turn right. Go past 'The Primrose Centre Hospice' and opposite, 'St Oswald's Park'. Just beyond, turn left on a path through trees and hedges. The field beyond touches on the edge of Aston Fields, part of Bromsgrove. Walk past a waymarker post and enter a playing field. It is best to turn sharp left at the end of this field, taking a green path through trees for about 100 yards to reach a lane. Turn right. Continue on an unmetalled drive which leads to a field. Go past a waymarker post into a larger field. Here, strictly, the right of way goes towards the railway line and then turns sharp left along the nearside hedgerow, but a diagonal crossing is traditional. Either way reaches a gate and waymarked stile. Go over and contour right beneath the farm on the hill to the left. Go over a stile on to the farm drive and follow it to a lane. Turn left to reach the Queens Head Inn, Stoke Pound.

From the inn, cross the canal bridge and turn sharp left to gain the towpath. The first lock is 'Tardebigge Bottom Lock'. Another 27 locks will be passed before the finish! The towpath offers excellent walking through serene country passing one or two canal side cottages and a reservoir before reaching the bridge used to cross the canal earlier on the walk. It only remains to pass under this to reach a cottage, and to retrace your steps up the bank to the **church**.

POINTS OF INTEREST:

St Bartholomew's Church, Tardebigge - The church stands on the site of an older building, records of worship on this spot going back to the Domesday Book. An old Norman church was demolished around 1775, when the tower collapsed, and the present church was built. The spire's topmost stone was removed during restoration in 1902 and now lies beside the altar.

REFRESHMENTS:

The Queens Head, Stoke Pound.
The Tardebigge Inn, Tardebigge.

Walk 62   SNODHILL AND VAGAR HILL   6m (9½km)

Maps: OS Sheets Landranger 161; Pathfinder 1039 and 1016.

A walk on the foothills of the Black Mountains, in very pleasant environs.

Start: At 323404, Snodhill Castle, near Dorstone.

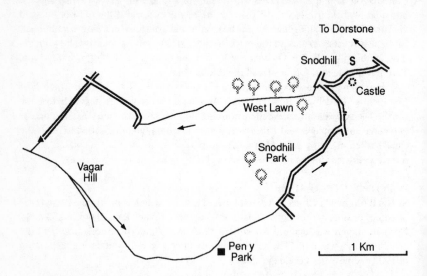

This is a well-found route starting from **Snodhill Castle** which although the OS map states only 'site of', actually still shows the remains of a keep constructed of thick stone walls. After an inspection of the site, return to the road and turn left, walking to a kind of T-junction, but with 3 possible ways adjoining. There is a 'No Through Road' at a 90° angle: take this, leftwards, and bear right around a bend to where it enters a band of tall trees, including oak and larch. Climb upwards, and where the road bends sharp left, leave it to carry on in the same direction, following a track. Ignore all other possibilities to reach a gate on to West Lawn Common. Keep left at first, then bear right at a fork to traverse round the slope of a hill. Presently, you will come to a stream by a gate. Cross and walk up to a lane. Turn right and follow the lane as it kinks left and then offers a straight section ending at a cross-roads. Turn left, passing a mast, to the right, and a trig. point (at 431 metres). Ahead is the bulk of Hay Bluff and the long skyline to Black Hill. The lane ends at a gate: go through and turn left to follow the broad top of Vagar Hill, with fine views over Herefordshire to the east and north. This is a bracing place, finely situated, though after rain it can be muddy.

Follow the ridge for a mile or so to reach a gate. Go through and bear left to follow a hedge to another gate. Go through and exchange sides of the hedgerow. Go past Pen y Parc, on the right, and continue to reach a gully, also on the right. Use this to reach a lane. Turn left and follow the lane, twisting right past a junction, on the right, and passing Snodhill Park, on the left. Now go steeply down, turning sharp left, then sharp right to return to Snodhill Castle.

POINTS OF INTEREST:

Snodhill Castle - The castle is 12th century and in a fine position overlooking the upper Golden Valley. It became ruinous about 1355, though it was semi-restored and used again during border conflicts in the 15th century. It finally met its end as a viable proposition during the Civil War.

REFRESHMENTS:

None on the walk, but there is a choice in nearby Dorstone.

EASTHAM $6^1/_2$m ($10^1/_2$km)
or $7^1/_2$m (12km)

Maps: OS Sheets Landranger 138; Pathfinder 973.
A scenic undulating walk.
Start: At 657687, in Eastham.

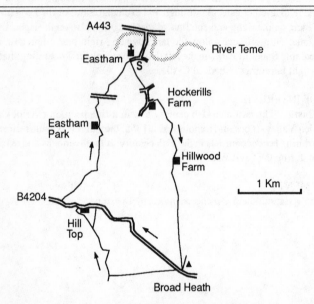

The **village church** is flanked by red-brick buildings from which a lane is followed
for 50 yards to a half-timbered cottage. Turn left over a broken fence/stile into a field.
Walk uphill to reach a gate. Now aim for an obvious red-brick house where turns left
and right lead to a gate. Continue beyond to reach a gate/stile on to a lane. Go straight
over and follow the signed lane for Highwood. Walk to a junction where there is a
signed track, on the left, for Hillwood Farm. Take this, passing an attractive building
(Hockerill's Farm). Beyond, swing right and ascend on a metalled lane to go through
Hillwood Farm. The route becomes a track: follow it up, then down a short dip into a
thin dell and along a stream by pheasant pens. Go past a derelict cottage, to the right,
beyond which the track degenerates to a thin path up the right edge of a field. At a
corner by a copse, go over a low fence and cross a stream. Now follow the left edge of

the next field, climbing steadily. Pass between two posts and go along a hedgerow, to the left, beyond which are a red-brick farmhouse and a large barn, to reach the B4204. Turn right to reach the Tally Ho Inn.

The shorter route, which is also useful if the ground this far has been wet, follows the road westwards. Although road walking is not for everyone, this is a quiet, scenic road offering fine views to the west. The routes rejoin at 'Hill Top', to the left.

For the longer route, go over the stile immediately on the inn's right wall and descend a valley across pasture, with excellent views towards Bringewod Chase and Titterstone Clee Hill. Pass a new plantation, to the right, and ascend, trending left where a stile gives access to a higher field. Go down a slight depression and then head towards a line of oak trees with a lateral hedge. Turn right by the trees, going down into another depression to cross the stream. Climb up the steep, muddy hillside to reach a ruin, presently being renovated. A possible diversion leftwards is drier. Turn left from the ruin, shortly going right where a route is seen heading for Hill Top. There is a way round Hill Top, taking a circuitous route leftwards, but this is hard to follow as it swings round the boundary and emerges on to the B4204. An alternative route takes the upper (right) boundary to reach the road further uphill.

The long and short routes rejoin here. Descend the road steeply to reach a bridleway on the right. Trend north-eastwards beneath the hill on the right, to reach ponds below a red-brick dwelling. Go across the bottom pond and through a gate. Go uphill slightly and then left over a domed field. Go through a gate where another pond, surrounded by poplar trees, is situated. Now aim for Eastham Park, swinging right, then left to reach a metalled lane. Turn right and, at the first bend, go through a gate into a field. Cross to a white gate a few yards uphill. Go through and walk along the field's right edge, going round by a knoll with two houses. Faithfully follow the field up and right to go through an old wooden gate. Ahead now is Eastham Church. Head for this, regaining the starting lane to complete the walk.

POINTS OF INTEREST:
The Church of St Peter and St Paul, Eastham - The key to the church can be obtained from the adjacent red-brick building. The church is 11th century, though a new tower (erected in 1830) has replaced the original wooden bell turret.

REFRESHMENTS:
The Tally Ho Inn, on the route.

Walk 65   **NINEVEH AND KYRE PARK**   6$\frac{1}{2}$m (10$\frac{1}{2}$km)

Maps: OS Sheets Landranger 138 or 149; Pathfinder 973 and 972.

A worthwhile route in relative solitude.

Start: At 623649, the Farmer's Boy Inn, Nineveh.

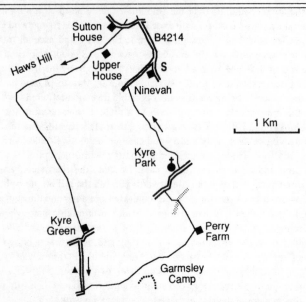

Walk north along the B4124, going round a sharp left-hand bend with a sign 'The Fulhams' opposite. Continue up the rise to where two iron gates sit opposite each other on the roadsides. Go left, then veer rightwards to reach a hedge corner and follow the hedge, with Sutton House some 150 yards away to the right. Go through a hedge gap on to a metalled drive and turn left. Swing right, with Upper House Farm on the left, then walk past a red cottage, enjoying views towards Titterstone Clee and High Vinnalls. Steadily ascend the drive to reach a detached red-brick building and outbuildings, to the right. Now take a left fork by a small copse to reach a gate. Beyond, follow a field edge by an isolated holly and then proceed straight ahead, going through several iron gates and passing an artificial pond, to the left. Descend slightly and go through a wooden gate on the left. Follow the right-hand field boundary to reach an iron gate just beyond a ruin. Go right and left through this, and then go through another iron gate into a long field. Go through a gap to another field, noting a plantation about 150 yards to the right. Dip slightly right to cross a horse jump by the trees and keep close to them to reach the clump of poplars ahead. Cross another horse jump, or go through a gate, and follow a line of oaks. Go through an iron gate and branch slightly right towards a wood ahead. Keep the wood on your right and go through hedge gaps between fields to reach a corrugated barn, to the left. Turn left through the yard just beyond and follow a drive to a lane. Turn right and climb the lane to its highest point, Just beyond there is a small, green reservoir: a few yards beyond this, turn left on to an obvious driveway.

Follow the drive to a partly timbered cottage and barns. There, take the left of two iron gates and go through to walk downhill through conifers. Across to the right, note the tree-covered hump of the ancient Garmsley Camp. The drive leaves the trees and continues to Perry Farm, to the right. Opposite this, go over a small stile into a paddock. Go past a dilapidated hut and cross a long field to its neck at the bottom. There, cross a stream and a waymarked stile. Swing left, then right following the hedge boundary. The next stile leads to a lane: turn right and walk past Pytts Cottages, to the right to reach the **church** at Kyre Park. Go through buildings to reach a stile with a walkway sign. Go over and trend left to the bottom corner of a wood where there is another waymarked stile. Go over and follow a field boundary to reach a gap into another field. Cross this alongside a fence. The next waymarked stile is crossed into a domed field. Climb this to reach an iron gate. Go through and walk along a large dwelling. Veer left and down to cross a wooden bridge over a stream. Beyond, maintain direction to reach the next waymarked stile. Go over one last stile and turn right along a lane to reach the B4214. Turn right to return to the start.

POINTS OF INTEREST:
Kyre Church - An interesting building, but usually locked. Dogged walkers will be able to gain access by ringing the Rev. Paul Lack (tel: 08867-286).

REFRESHMENTS:
The Farmer's Boy Inn, at the start.

Walk 66   **BROMYARD AND THE EDVINS**   7m (11km)

Maps: OS sheets Landranger 149; Pathfinder 995.

Quiet walking connecting two isolated and interesting churches.
Start: At 653548, the free car park by the Conquest Theatre in
Bromyard.

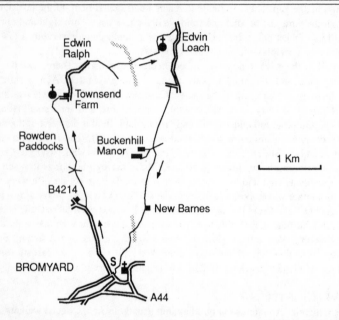

Turn right out of the car park and go along the B4214, to cross the River Frome. Not
far beyond, the road bends left. There, take the bridleway to the right, passing a large
bungalow, left, to reach a stile. Go over and follow the left side of a field, near a
brook, to reach a stile. Go straight on, passing a caravan park, left, then going over
another stile. Maintain direction to reach a stile to the left of a part-timbered red
cottage. A walking sign points diagonally right: follow it downhill to another stile.
Go over and keep to the left edge of a field to reach a bridge. Cross, go over a stile in
a corner and immediately go over another and follow the right-hand edge of a field to
reach a stile in the bottom right corner. Beyond, cross boggy ground, a bridge over a
stream and two stiles, then ascend the right edge of a field bordered by hawthorn

hedges to reach a gate. Look back to see the Bromyard Downs and the abutting Malvern Hills. Go diagonally left across a field to reach a stile into the Church of St Michael, **Edwyn Ralph**.

Exit through a smart gate by an old green lamp standard and turn sharp right down a metalled lane, going around the attractive Townend Farm. Two paths cross the lane: ignore these, continuing past the half-timbered buildings of Brickhouse Farm. Beyond, the lane is unmetalled and goes through more open scenery. Swing right, away from a copse, and after another 100 yards you will find a gate on the left. The church spire of Edvin Loach dominates the skyline ahead, whilst far left there is a glimpse of Titterstone Clee. Descend to a cottage, go left of its yard and then right, going down and crossing a bridge over a stream. Go up a steep, central line to reach a stile. Go over and walk to a cottage. Walk parallel to its drive, reaching it over a stile. At a T-junction turn left along a tree-lined way, passing a large house. Just beyond, go through a gate and cross an enclosure to a small gate into **Edvin Loach** churchyard. Walk to a T-junction and turn right along a lane, going as far as a house with a tower. There, turn right and follow a track to a gate. Turn left down the field beyond, go over a stile and continue down, going across a bridge over a stream. Go up over a crest and down towards Buckenhill Manor. Go round its left-hand boundary going through a wooden gate next to a white iron one. Follow waymarkers over stiles and fields, passing New Barnes Farm, to the left. Bear diagonally right across two fields to reach a gate. Beyond, cross a bridge over a stream. Go over a waymarked stile and a fence aiming for Bromyard Church ahead. Cross a packhorse bridge over a river, and go past an abandoned black and white building. Cross a lane and go up the hill by an old school. Go along Church Lane into Cruxwell Street, to the right. Now pass the White Horse Inn and return to the start.

POINTS OF INTEREST:

Edwyn Ralph/Edvin Loach – The names Edwyn and Edvin may derive from Gedwen, an area once owned by the Norman Osbern Fitzrichard. This fell into the hands of the Ralphs and the DeLoqes giving the villages their second names. Inside Edwyn Ralph Church are seven monumental figures – the finest in a Herefordshire church.

REFRESHMENTS:

The White Horse Inn, Bromyard.
There are also other possibilities in Bromyard.

Walk 67   **WOOLHOPE AND SOLLERS HOPE**   7m (11km)

Maps: OS Sheets Landranger 149; Pathfinder 1040 and 1041.

A walk that is pleasantly different.

Start: At 612357, the car park, Woolhope Church.

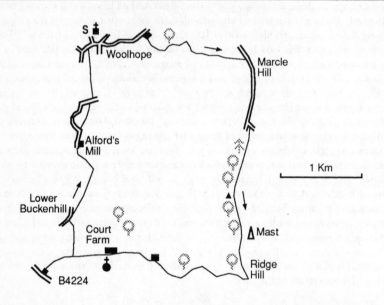

Leave the car park along a path to the Crown Inn. Take the lane, left, and go east, downhill, ignoring the road, right, to Sollers Hope. Reach the valley bottom, by the Butchers Arms, taking a lane to the right before it. Follow the lane to find a signed path on a bend. Keep straight on, climbing towards woodland. The lane becomes unsurfaced: continue, then go through a gate on to open hillside, with sweeping views to the right. The path levels out: head towards a line of trees to reach, at their left end, a gate and stile. Beyond, the path descends along the wood edge, goes over a stile and crosses a valley. Keep to the hedge to the left, go through a gate and continue to a lane by a cottage. Go right on the only route over Marcle Hill. The road forks by a Marcle Hill Picnic Site sign: go over the obvious stepped-stile and follow the edge of Ridge Hill. Go over two more stiles, then kink right and left to go over a waymarked stile to

130

reach the trig point, with a radio mast just ahead. Beyond the mast beautiful views open up to the right. A stile, to the left, takes the path the other side of a hedge. Now descend over steps and a stile and turn right along a bridleway. Descend to a fold and a stone barn, to the right, then keep straight on to follow the wood edge, on the right, to reach a lane. Follow this to a left-hand bend where a stile, to the right, leads into a field. Go down to a gap in the corner by a stream, continuing to a gate on to a lane, opposite a long stone barn. Go left and immediately right through a gate. Bear left, following a stream, and go over a stile by a tree. Aim for the timbered Court Farm passing it by way of a stile to reach **St Michael's Church, Sollers Hope**.

Leave the church grounds through a gate, cross a bridge over a stream and another stile in a hedge, by a prominent non-prickly holly. Go over an awkward double stile and cross a field to reach two stiles in the left-hand corner. Another stile leads round a cottage on to a drive which is followed to Gurney's Oak inn, on the B4224. Retrace your steps to the last cottage and go left over a stile and downhill along the field edge which forms the boundary to the cottage. Descend to a stream. Go through a gate and turn immediately right over a bridge. Now go diagonally left towards a farm building. Gates and a stile lead to a lane past this fine building dated 1592. After 40 yards go right over a signed stile and aim just left of a tree to find a stile in the middle of the fence. Beyond a rise, dip down to a gate, crossing the next field to reach a stile. Now aim for the black and white cottage ahead (Alford's Mill). Go along a farm track and 100 yards beyond a barn, to the right, go through a blue gate to the right. Go over a rail and a stile, then use two stiles to cross a lane. Go slightly right across a field to reach a bridge. Go over an obvious stile and cross fields to reach a lane back into Woolhope. Turn right, then left to return to the church car park.

POINTS OF INTEREST:
St Michael's Church, Sollers Hope - This fine 14th-century building was probably financed by Robert, brother of Dick Whittington.

REFRESHMENTS:
The Crown Inn, Woolhope.
The Gurney's Oak Inn, on the B4224.

Walk 68   WEST MALVERN AND CRADLEY   7m (11km)

Maps: OS Sheets Landranger 150; Pathfinder 1018.

Picturesque country walking west of the Malvern Hills.

Start: At 766472, in West Malvern.

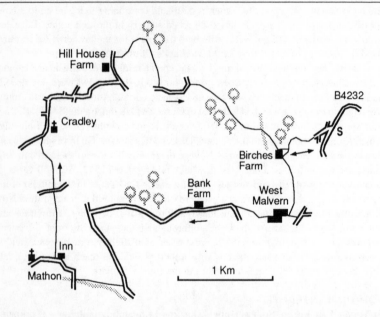

Go south on the B4232 towards the Lamb Inn, taking a road, signed West Malvern OE Centre, to the right just before it. Go over a cross-roads (by sign to West Malvern Playing Fields) continuing downhill to pass the buildings of the Outdoor Education Centre. Continue along the, now unmetalled, lane to reach Birches Farm. Go through a gate, to the left, and along an obvious track beside trees to reach a gate into the next field. Turn right to a farm. Go straight through this to find a stile by a thicket. The next stile, in just a few yards, leads to a field with pretty views ahead. Go right, along a track, then leave it to go down to the corner of a square wood. Take a track beside the wood to reach a waymarked stile on to a lane. Walk ahead, passing a cottage to reach Bank Farm. Kink through the farm, ignoring a waymarked path, to the left, to go straight on through a waymarked gate and along an unmetalled track, with good views to the left and a wood on the right. Go through the wood, emerging to swing right, across open grassland, then left, downhill, to a half-timbered cottage. There are two stiles on the right beyond this cottage: either leads on a gated track which is followed to Quabbs Head Cottage. About 400 yards beyond, turn sharp right, by another half-timbered cottage, on to a signed path. Cross fields, with a stream to the left, and stiles to reach a stile on to a lane. Turn right into Mathon, perhaps visiting **St John's Church**.

Some yards west of the Cliffe Arms there is a path to the right. Take this, going across a bridge over a stream. Go straight across a field to reach a stile. Go over and cross a field to a gap into the next field. Cross to reach a gate on to a drive and follow it past Churchfields House and into Cradley. Follow the lane through the village, perhaps visiting **St James' Church**. Walk past tiny Clematis Cottage and the Post Office, continuing to reach more modern houses. Opposite these go right, following a sign for Church Stile Farm. Go past the farm, continuing to reach a T-junction. Turn left, passing Hill House, on the left, and, at the end of a double bend, go right through a gate. Go through another after a few yards and walk with a hedge on your left and hawthorn thickets on your right. Go through a gate with a pond on the right and, just beyond, either turn right into a field or go into the wood and turn sharp right on to a track. Either way leads to two gates (one wooden, one iron) at an angle to each other. A thin grass path beyond leads to two gates across a track. Take a thin path towards a red house where another gate leads to a lane. Turn left. Soon, take a bridleway on the right and go uphill through woodland to reach a cross-ways. Go slightly right to reach a waymarked path that leads steeply downhill, leaving the wood through a gate into a field. A second gate allows the descent to continue to a tiny stream and a third gate. Aim just left of Birches Farm to cross a stile to reach the track to the Outdoor Centre. Now retrace the outward route back to the start.

POINTS OF INTEREST:
St John's Church, Mathon - The yew in the churchyard is thought to be over 1000 years old.
St James' Church, Cradley - Be sure to look for the length of Saxon carved frieze on the north wall, and the medieval lych gate.

REFRESHMENTS:
The Lamb Inn, near the start.
The Cliffe Arms, Mathon.

Walk 69   GARWAY AND GARWAY HILL   7m (11km)

Maps: OS Sheets Landranger 161; Pathfinder 1064.

The epitome of 'the back of beyond' with a hill offering a superb viewpoint.

Start: At 466227, the Garway Moon Inn, Garway Common.

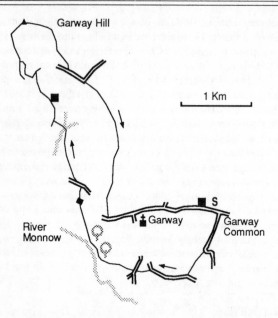

Walk to a phone box and turn right opposite, on a road signed for Skenfrith and Abergavenny. The road crosses the open common to reach a sharp left turn. Here, go through a gate, right, and immediately go left, hugging the hedge to pass a new house. At the side of its garage is a gate into a field. Follow the field's left edge down to an awkward gate/stile. Go over and turn right along a lane. Walk between the buildings of Garway Court, a working farm, and on the next sharp right bend, go left through a gate and down a field. Keep just left of a cottage in the valley, go through a gate and down steps to a lane. Cross to a signed gate into a field. Go over a brow to reach a signed stile. Go over this and another stile after 40 yards. Turn right along a track beneath trees. Cross a field to reach a gate. Go to the right of the farm ahead, going over a stile to reach a stone barn. Go left into the farm area, then turn right on a drive and follow it to a lane. Turn left. After 100 yards, turn right through a gate and follow a farm track along field edges, crossing two awkward gates and going over a stream. Strike left and uphill to reach a gate or gap in a hedge. About 70 yards beyond go right on to a track, bearing left by farm buildings. Go past a red detached house to reach a T-junction. Turn left to skirt a property within trees to the right and after 150 yards swing right on to a track. Leave this immediately to veer right up a green path between bracken on the slopes of Garway Hill. This is not a right of way, but there are several ways up this hill which are unrestricted. Reach the summit of Garway Hill with its tremendous views of the Black Mountains, Blorenge, Ysgyryd Fawr, the distant Radnor Forest and Hergest Ridge, even Titterstone Clee. Then gaze round to the Malverns, May Hill, the hills of the Wye Valley and Forest of Dean and the closely intervening Graig Syfryddin to complete a full circle.

From the summit strike right down a wide green path, and, after a few hundred yards, take a track bearing right through bracken and heading down towards a ruin. Look for a gate on its left. Go through and follow the right field edge to a stile and bank. Go over on to a lane and turn left. Walk past the first cottage on the right, then go over a stile on the right and down a field. Go over a footbridge and stile in a dip and then rightwards to reach another stile. Take a middle course across a field to reach a stile. Go over and follow the right-hand hedge to reach a stile on the right. Go over and turn left along the other side of the hedge to reach a gate some yards right of the bottom boundary. Take the left edge of the next field and go through a gate, with a farm on the right, on to a track. Turn left and walk to the next turning on the right where a short detour visits **St Michael's Church, Garway**. Return to the lane and turn right back to Garway Common and the start of the walk.

POINTS OF INTEREST:

St Michael's Church, Garway - The church dates from 1180 when Garway was granted to the Knights Templar who protected pilgrims to the Holy Land. The building once had a round nave, architecturally influenced by churches in the Holy Land. Only the chancel arch remains of this.

REFRESHMENTS:
The Garway Moon Inn, Garway.

Walk 70   LONGTOWN AND HATTERRALL HILL   7m (11km)

Maps: OS Sheets Landranger 161; Pathfinder 1063.

A fine hill walk on to Offa's Dyke Path.

Start: At 325287, the lay-by near Longtown Post Office.

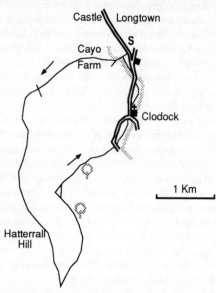

Walk south and turn right, at a white corner cottage, into a 'No Through Road'. Cross the Olchon Brook and, immediately beyond, go over a stile, half-right, bearing right, beyond, to reach a gate. Go half-right over a stile for 100 yards to reach another stile, then walk 200 yards to cross yet another stile, and a ditch. Go through a gate and turn left through the yard of Cayo Farm. Go through two gates into a field and cross this, and the next field, close to the right edge. In the top corner, two tree trunks offer a way over a fence. Bear left across a field to reach a gate. Beyond, a green track leads through another gate and crosses a lateral track. About 50 yards beyond, go diagonally left on a path up the scarp slope, joining the Offa's Dyke Path at the ridge. Turn left along the Path, passing overgrown quarry workings to reach Hatterrall Hill. As you walk the view ahead is of Sugar Loaf, while below and right is the Vale of Ewyas and

Llanthony Abbey. Beyond the high point descend steadily, the view ahead now being of Ysgyryd Fawr almost end on.

At a signpost (in both Welsh, near side, and English) bear left on a path that, in summer, can be difficult to follow through the bracken. A fence and hedges, with farmhouses in clumps of pines beyond, are a useful landmark. Walk along the base of the steep scarp of the hill to go through two gates 50 yards apart. There is no clear path now, so either go across to gate in the far corner. Go through, turn right and right again to follow a track down to a farm, or, turn right down the field to a gate, trend left down the next field to another gate and head for the white-trimmed gable end of the same farm. Bear right by the farm on to a concrete drive. Pass a second farm, left, continuing to a T-junction. Go over the waymarked stile opposite and cross a field to a corner stile and footbridge. Aim for the far corner of the next field to reach footbridge, crossing the field beyond to reach a lane and the Cornewall Arms. Go over a stone stile into the very 'populated' graveyard to inspect **St Clydawg's Church**. Go over a stile on the far right and follow a path beside the River Monnow. Cross two fields, then go through a gate and bear left away from the river. Cross a green avenue and a stile and bear left to reach two stiles that lead to a road. Now either turn right back to **Longtown**, or turn right and immediately left across a stone slab over the Ochlon Brook. Now cross a field to a stile, go over and turn right into a football field. Go left along its edge, through a gate, then through another and turn right on a lane. At a junction, turn left back to the post office.

POINTS OF INTEREST:

St Clydawg's Church, Clodock – This church is the only one in the world dedicated to this saint! The church was founded in 520AD, though the present building dates from the 12th century. Note the excellent 17th century pews and wooden balcony and an 8th century slab (inscribed in Latin) to the wife of a certain Guindda.

Longtown Castle - The castle has the earliest example of a round keep in England.

REFRESHMENTS:

The Crown Inn, Longtown.
The Cornewall Arms,Clodock.
There is also a Post Office/store in Longtown.

Walk 71 BROAD HEATH AND WOLFERLOW 7m (11km)

Maps: OS Sheets Landranger 138 or 149; Pathfinder 973.

An interesting walk below and along a broad scarp.

Start: At 663655, the Tally Ho Inn, Broad Heath.

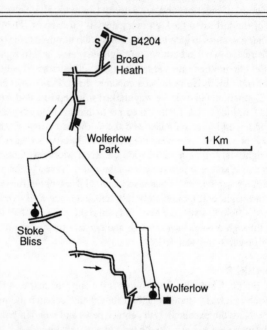

From the inn which commands fine views, walk south to a T-junction. Turn right along a lane, going downhill to a junction. Turn left (signed Stoke Bliss) to reach Woodstock Bower Farm, to the right. There, go over a stile and head diagonally right to go through a gate. Bear right towards two oaks. Beyond go through a gate/gap and descend steeply to the far corner of a wood. Go through a gate. Pass a ruined barn to reach a waymarked post descending as indicated. This section is difficult with a steep bank and a thin overgrown path. Another waymarked post takes you over a drop and a stile. Cross a track and continue to a bridge with a blue arrow waymarker into a field. Keep left of a green gate: the right of way is across the field, not on the more obvious track to the right of a hedge. Go through a gate on to a lane. Turn right. Ahead is a bridleway by trees and a gate: take this, it may be muddy, to reach another gate.

Turn left along a field hedge to reach a gate, then follow the right-hand side of a hedge to reach a wooden gate. Cross the field beyond, going through a gap into the next field. Beyond the next gate the spire of Stoke Bliss Church can be seen ahead. Half-way down the field, go through a gate on the left and follow a thin, awkward path to reach a T-junction of paths. Turn left, then right through a gate on to a track to a lane. Follow the track to a lane and turn right to visit **St Peter's Church**.

From a yard opposite the church, on the corner, take a curving, descending track into a small valley. The track now ascends and goes diagonally right under cables to reach a blue gate. Go through and walk past sheds, left, following a track which bears right to reach a lane. Turn left along the lane, snaking uphill. After the fourth bend, you are on level ground. Take a drive to the right, near Upper House Farm which is set back, on the right. After 150 yards, turn left along a field path, aiming for the church at Wolferlow by keeping along a hedgerow. The church can be visited, but this is risky as parts of the roof are in poor repair.

Beyond the church, go left along a drive by a bungalow and then go left up a lane for 250 yards before going over a stile on the right. Cross the field beyond to reach another, crossing this one by swapping sides of the hedge. Now keep left of a long strip of trees to reach a gate and a track. The track zig-zags to the left. Do not go as far as a farm yard: instead, go through a gap into a field and bear slightly left to its top corner where trees form the boundary. Go through a gate and follow the edge of the next field to reach a gate. Follow a wider track, with good views to the left, to reach another track and, eventually, a lane near farm buildings. Now retrace the outward route, turning right, then left to return to the start.

POINTS OF INTEREST:
St Peter's Church, Stoke Bliss - The church was built in about 1200 by Matilda de Mortimer. The 13th century Lady Chapel is dedicated as a childrens' church. Note the interesting memorial tablets to members of the Pytts family.

REFRESHMENTS:
The Tally Ho Inn, Broad Heath.

Maps: OS Sheets Landranger 138; Pathfinder 952.
Varied scenery and three pretty villages.
Start: At 690716, in Mamble village.

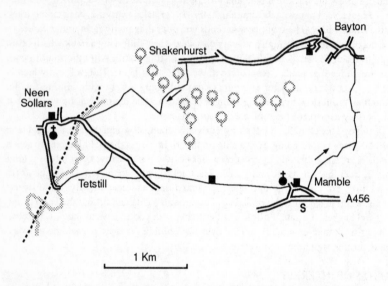

About 20 yards east of, and opposite, the village hall is a track. Take this, going through a gate into a field. Follow a hedge, but ignore a stile to the left, bearing slightly right along a fence to go over the next stile. Trend left for 50 yards, then turn right along a hedge and go over a small stile. In the next corner there is a stream and a waymarked stile. Cross the stream along a worn way into the next field and head for a ruin on the skyline. Go over the brow and go straight downhill to reach a waymarked stile beneath the tree line. Go over and turn left to reach a bridge over the stream. Climb steeply up the edge of the dell on the right to reach a field and follow its left-hand edge to reach a gate. Cross a stream on a track and follow a path, left, across a field to reach a lane. Go left to a T-junction in Bayton. Turn left, then right along the lane to Shakenhurst and Ninevah. Now take a lane to the left signed to the church. Follow the path which bears right around St Bartholomew's Church and then go diagonally right down a field to reach a metalled lane. Turn left, passing a solitary black and white cottage. Ahead there is a stately looking house: before reaching this, go left beyond a clump of fenced trees going down beside a neck of woodland to reach a stile, to the right, on to a track from the right. Turn left, go over a stream and immediately turn right, passing a large pond, left. Go straight on by piles of timber, beyond which the track curves left, but then very sharply right. Although not an official right of way, the track is more obvious and convenient to follow as it snakes through a gap/gate to meet another track (the right of way) at a T-junction. Turn left, go under electricity cables and through a gate. Bear right, downhill, by a bordered copse and descend a grassy corridor to reach a gate. Follow the drive beyond into **Neen Sollars**, a village which is actually in Shropshire.

Go left from the village inn, following the lane to two large, detached houses and taking the drive alongside them. Cross a bridge over a railway line and note a very attractive mill and weir to the left. Cross a river, swing left and curve round towards two red brick dwellings and barn, Go over a tiny stile, to the left, just before them, go through a gate and climb a field, keeping to the hedge on the right, to reach a gate. Go past a modern barn, right, and through a gap by a detached brick house where its drive reaches Neenshilltop Cottage. Turn right along a lane. Take the first track on the left, then, after a few yards, bear right to reach a stile underneath electricity cables. The next pair of stiles span a ditch: keep to the line of the cables to go over another stile into a paddock. Cross to another paddock, with a farmhouse to the left, go through a gate and over a stile. Cross the centre of the next field aiming for Mamble Church. Cross two fields and a ditch, then climb to reach a waymarked stile. Go over on to a grassy alley and follow it into Mamble. Now take the short step back to the start.

POINTS OF INTEREST:
Neen Sollars – The village name derives from the names of two Norman families joined by marriage around 1200.

REFRESHMENTS:
The Railway Tavern, Neen Sollars.
The Wheatsheaf Inn, Bayton.

Walk 73   QUEENSWOOD COUNTRY PARK AND WESTHOPE HILL

7m (11km)

Maps: OS Sheets Landranger 149; Pathfinder 994.

An arboretum with countless species, then wide open walking with distant horizons.

Start: At 506516, Queenswood Country Park Visitor Centre.

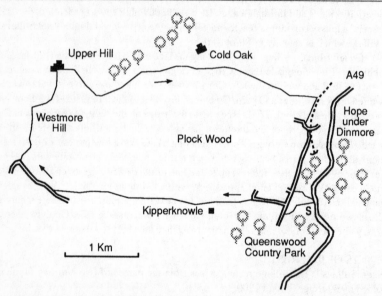

Go directly between the buildings of the Visitor Centre and the café on a track called 'The Lime Way' to reach a gate signed 'The Autumn Garden'. Go through and kink right and left to follow a hardcore road through the trees. Turn right at a T-junction and after about 150 yards take a major driveway on the left. Go past a bungalow to reach a corner where there is an iron gate and a walkway sign. Proceed ahead along the field edge, with fine views to the right over a wooded valley. Ahead there are large, isolated buildings: veer slightly right of these to pass an oak tree and reach a stile. Go over on to a wide drive by the Hereford Shooting School. A red-brick dwelling, Kipperknowle, is down to the right. The drive bears away right, downhill. Do not follow it: instead, go straight on through a gap and over a stile into a field. Cross a ditch, by way of a gate and path (of sorts) and bear right to reach a stile. Go over and continue to reach a stile on the curve of the next field. Go over and head for a lateral hedge in which there is another stile. Go over and cross a rough pasture to reach a wide track. Turn right, following the track through an iron gate in a hedge. Now hard-cored, the track passes a couple of dwellings to reach a T-junction. Turn right, as signed, on to Westhope Common. Go past two properties on the left, turning left around the final property's boundary. Continue for several hundred yards, then turn right on to a track right which, eventually, leads down to the far right-hand corner of the common. Go through a band of trees, keeping right of a farm, to reach a gate on to a lane. Go along the lane, then bear right at a fork by Rose Cottage, following the track to reach a stile to the left of a gate. Go over and head for a gate that leads into a dry shallow valley. Now follow a field edge, going over two stiles. Beyond the second is a path: turn left along it.

The path passes close to a prominent long wood. Go over a stile and bear right to reach another in a fence. Now follow a thin, but well defined path that crosses fields and stiles before going under cables to reach a stile in a hedge. Go over and trend rightwards down to another stile, with a barn to the left. Go over this and further stiles and fields to reach a good track which is followed past pig sheds. Now veer off left, cross a stile and go downhill towards a railway. Turn right along a field to reach a drive at a property. Follow the drive to a lane. Follow a lane to reach a railway bridge. Now turn up the lane or cross the adjacent field. Pass a horse route on the left. Now just beyond a property named 'The Paddocks' there is a driveway on the right. Opposite on the left is a fenced gap: go through this into the woods. Take a right fork immediately and you will soon find the 'Old Road' in the **Arboretum**. Turn left and then go rightwards back to the Visitor Centre.

POINTS OF INTEREST:
Arboretum (Queenswood Country Park) – The arboretum has a splendid variety of native and foreign trees, including California Redwoods. A guide book and a free map are available at the Visitor Centre.

REFRESHMENTS:
The café at the Visitor Centre.

Walk 74   A FOWNHOPE CIRCUIT   7m (11km)

Maps: OS Sheets Landranger 149; Pathfinder 1040.
An excellent mixture of river walking and wooded hills.
Start: At 578344, the New Inn, Fownhope.

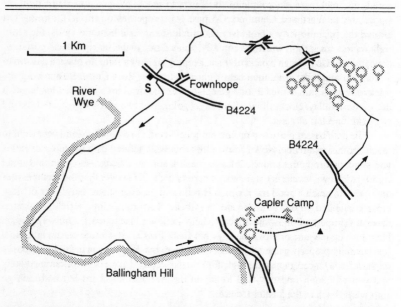

Walk towards the church to find, after about 100 yards, a walkway sign on the left pointing into an alley opposite. Follow the alley to a stile into a field. Go left and cross another stile into a field at the back of the houses in Fownhope. Turn right to the playing fields and go through an iron gate by a sewerage plant. Head towards the River Wye, visible ahead, to reach a stone cottage. A few yards beyond this, go over a stile in the hedge to the left. There is a route straight on along a riverside path, but a recent landslide has meant that, though it is passable, it is an adventurous - not to say dangerous and tortuous - passage. Therefore, head up the field behind the trees on the very steep slope down to the river. Go through a gate and descend easily to regain the river bank. Follow a huge sweeping bend of the Wye, passing the two black and white houses of Ballingham Hill on the opposite bank. Stay with the river path, going past the small enclosure of a stone cottage by way of a waymarked stile. Soon after, cross a brook by a wooden bridge and head for Capler Camp, the wooded hill ahead. Go past a cottage on the left, beyond which a stile gives access to a wood. Turn sharp left and climb a thin path to meet a lateral track. A walkway sign points right along it: either take this track and then a steep path back leftwards and uphill to meet a road, or gain height more steadily and then turn left, then right on to the road. Follow the road to reach a bungalow where the Wye Valley Walk goes left up a drive through larch trees. Follow the Way, which is well waymarked through the woods, veering right then opening out to the fortifications of **Capler Camp**. Go past a barn and cottage, trend slightly right by a waymarked post, going over the stile beyond and going down steeply via steps. Exit from the trees and go past a white cottage and barns to reach a waymarked post and stile. Go left to reach a gate. Go through and turn right along a drive to reach the B4224.

Turn left for 100 yards, then go right along a drive by a property. Now look for a waymarker post which gives the line along the right-hand hedge, heading down to a farmhouse. Skirt this by way a stile in the hedge and head down to a gap. Cross the stream beyond and go over a waymarked stile immediately to the left. Go over another stile about 70 yards further on and turn left to reach a cottage. Some yards beyond this there is a stile into a wood: go over and follow the path beyond. This trends rightwards, then bears left to reach an iron gate and a stile. Just to the left, in a clearing, is a modern property: trend right up to a stile in a corner, with a white house opposite. Take the waymarked driveway to this property and, in a few yards, bear left on a waymarked track. Kink right and left over a stile and go along an interesting woodland ridge, with a fine viewpoint over Fownhope. Go straight on at a path crossroads (following the Wye Valley Walk). Walk through excellent woodland passing a cottage and, further on, reaching an abandoned (?) cottage, with red-tiled roof, in the trees to the left. Some yards beyond, turn left acutely on a path, following it to reach a post waymarked with two arrows. Turn right, downhill. Go round the base of a tree covered hill, to the right, and, soon, Fownhope is seen ahead. Follow the walkway signs rightwards through an estate, passing a school to emerge on the main road very near your starting point.

POINTS OF INTEREST:
Capler Camp – Another of Herefordshire's numerous Iron Age hillforts.

REFRESHMENTS:
The New Inn, Fownhope.

Walk 75 STOKE PRIOR AND MARSTON STANNETT 7m (11km)
Maps: OS Sheets Landranger 149; Pathfinder 994.
A walk to 'the back of beyond' in rolling countryside.
Start: At 522566, in Stoke Prior village.

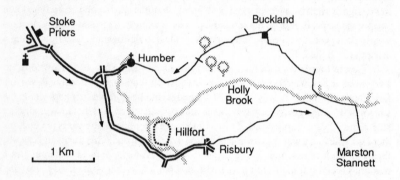

Having inspected the village, with its fine and historic half-timbered dwellings and church, head south-east along the road to reach a cross-roads. Parking for one car is available here if you wish to avoid the road walking. Go straight over and continue to reach a slanting T-junction. The right of way over a stile opposite has disappeared and no way now seems possible beyond the first field, so follow the lane southwards bending round and dipping down by Risbury hillfort and Risbury Court, passing an attractive garden lake reflecting a cottage. Turn left at a junction signed Risbury and Pencombe and walk into Risbury. Turn left at a sign for Poplands. About twenty yards further on turn right on to a bridleway. Take a middle course across a field, then walk past the line of trees ahead to reach a small gate on the right. Go through this and another just beyond, cross a track and climb beside a field hedge. Go through an iron gate and then go right through a smaller gate. In the field beyond, trend rightwards away from the hedge to cross a stream. Cross two more fields with thin hedges, go down into a dip and follow a line of trees and a hedge to reach a gap. Go through and cross scrub, passing some new trees to reach a small iron gate. Go through and take a track uphill to reach a cottage with a black barn. Beyond, a good track is followed into Marston Stannett.

Go through this fine old collection of houses and farm buildings and turn left beyond a paved courtyard. Turn left again at a fork with an iron gate beyond. Go through a green gate and follow a good track, turn left at a diagonal iron gate. Now go downhill to reach a gate. Beyond, the route is steeper, going through young trees to reach a fence/stile at the bottom left. Go left on a track which follows the Holly Brook. Go through two fields, glimpsing the cottage on the hill, to the left, passed earlier. Go through a gate into a field and ford a stream. The ford is usually straightforward, but after prolonged rain can be tricky. Go right and then left, on an undefined route up a field. Cross the next field to reach an iron gate. Go through and follow the left hedge, with a brand new barn several hundred yards away to the right, to reach a lateral bridleway. Turn left, passing a farm to reach a better track which leads to Buckland. Turn right, then left around its perimeter. Take the obvious track through farm buildings. Now ignore a track bearing right to go straight on into a field. Go past a plantation on the right and cross a field with a wood about 150 yards away to the left. Cross the next field to reach a wooden gate adjacent to a ditch. Go through and follow the right-hand edge to reach a bridge on the right. Take this across a stream continuing to reach an iron gate. Go through and keep right of farm buildings and a yard to reach a lane. Turn left into Humber. The isolated **church** here is well worth a visit. After your visit, go through the churchyard, heading leftwards to go through two gates on to a lane. Follow this to a cross-roads. Go over and follow the lane opposite to reach the outward route at the next cross-roads. Now retrace your steps back to Stoke Prior.

POINTS OF INTEREST:
St Mary the Virgin Church, Humber - The keys to this fine church are available from Humber Grange, the adjacent, large house. The church is typically Herefordshire Norman with an attractive spire and some fine old windows.

REFRESHMENTS:
TheLamb Inn, Stoke Prior.

Walks 76 & 77   OVERBURY AND BREDON HILL   7m (11km)
or 9m (14¹⁄₂km)

Maps: OS Sheets Landranger 150; Pathfinder 1042.
Two pretty villages linked by a good walk over Bredon Hill.
Start: At 957374, St Faith's Church, Overbury.

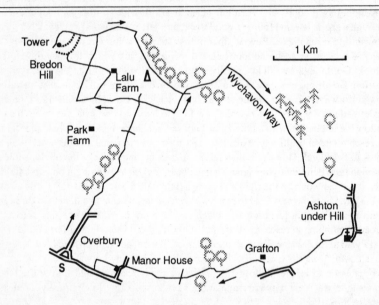

Walk along the lane from **St Faith's Church,** passing Overbury Court's large gates
and going right by some pretty cottages. Turn left at a T-junction, following a lane as
far as three garages and a right turn. Do not take this: instead, go straight on along a
'No Through Road' sign and veer right up a track flanking woods to the left. Go into
and out of the woods, then cross a track leading to a farm to the left. Turn right and
left here, going through a gate. Continue to reach a plantation to the right.

The shorter route turns right away from the plantation, following a good path,
from which there are excellent views as far as the Black Mountains, past spaced pines
to reach a corner. Turn left and go through two gates to rejoin the longer route.

The longer route takes the track to the left, going over a cross-roads and then
through a gate on the right. Turn sharp left and follow a wall to reach a clump of

148

pines. Turn left here for a short detour to Bredon Hill. Follow the left edge of the pines, aiming for the trees ahead. Turn right, then left, around their boundary to rejoin the shorter route near a gate (with a Wychavon Way sign) into a wood. Descend to the next gate and follow the path beyond to reach a stile on the right. Go over a brow and dip leftwards to reach a stile in a fence. Go over and follow a wire fence past a pool and some big trees. Go round a sheep fold and pass a cattle grid, right, and a field, left. Walk along the edge of a plantation, left, and go through a gate. Bear right to head for a small gate by an iron gate and follow the double track beyond across a rough meadow. The track becomes hardcored: ignore a waymarked gate up and right to go through two iron gates by a lonely house and paddocks to reach a metalled drive. Go left, then right and downhill past some fine cottages into Ashton-under-Hill. Turn right at the T-junction, admiring the lovely thatched cottages opposite the Star Inn (dated 1742).

From the inn, walk to **St Barbara's Church**, go up a path and through the lych gate to reach a gate into a field. Go left, then bear right at an iron gate and walkway sign. Go through and bear right to reach a corner iron gate. Follow the track beyond, forking left, and following the left side of a hedge to cross a footbridge over a stream into a field. Go through a gate on to a lane. Walk ahead, ignoring a path to the right to reach a left bend. Here, bear right by an ornate gable on to a path. Go through an iron gate, to the right, to avoid a thatched cottage on the left. Go through a gate into a field and cross to a stile. Go over and turn left to walk beside a hedge and willow trees. Bear left to a square enclosure and upturned stone. Now contour across two rough fields, linked by a stile, to reach a stile into a wood. Exit the wood and walk past a group of poplars, and some firs to the left, following a good track. In the next field, go right and left through a gate then go over a stile and through a gate to reach a high boundary wall. Bear right on to a lane. Go over a step stile into a paddock and cross to another into an orchard. Go across and take a wide path across a field into a group of firs. Turn left through them to reach a stile. Go over and turn right back to Overbury.

POINTS OF INTEREST:

St Faith's Church, Overbury - St Faith was burned at a stake for her beliefs and is depicted in the north aisle window holding a palm and grate. The font dates from around 1150, while some of the nave seating is 15th century.

St Barbara's Church, Ashton-under-Hill - The church, with a fine 14th century porch, is one of only two English churches dedicated to this saint.

REFRESHMENTS:

The Star Inn, Ashton-under-Hill.

There is also a small store in Overbury.

Walk 78   ALVECHURCH AND ROWNEY GREEN   7m (11km)

Maps: OS Sheets Landranger 139; Pathfinder 975.

A walk maintaining interest through rolling countryside.

Start: At 028726, the free car park near centre of Alvechurch.

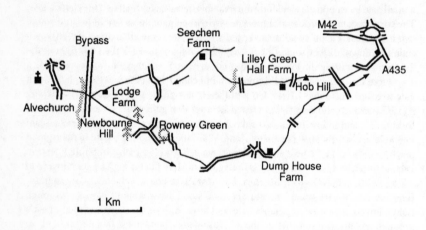

Walk along Swan Street, the old A441, going south past a nursery and turning left on to a drive signed Lodge Farm. Cross the River Arrow and kink uphill under the new A441 (the Alvechurch bypass) to reach a waymarked stile, to the right. Go over and cross fields, walking uphill and aiming for a wooded hilltop. Go into the wood, through a group of firs, to reach several ways. Take the widest one, which is more or less straight ahead. Cross a lane and, opposite, trend downhill on another lane. Just as the gradient steepens, go left and up through a gap to reach a waymarked stile into a wood. Go through the wood and turn right on to a lane. Take the second turning left, by a Neighbourhood Watch sign. Enter the grounds of a white cottage and go right across its gravel yard. Now follow a hedge/gully, bending sharp left after a few yards to go across the bottom of a garden and cross a bridge over a brook into a field. Go left, following the line of the brook and then crossing it by way of waymarked stiles

150

and a bridge. Go right to reach a stile. Go over and turn left along a lane to reach its junction with Lilley Green Road. Turn left, then right into Dump House Lane, following it to Dump House Farm, an attractive period cottage dating from the late 18th or early 19th century. Ignore a path going right and go through the yard on a thin path. Continue through trees to reach a stile on the left. Go over and bear right to cross a footbridge over a stream. Go over the stile beyond into a field. Keep close to the stream, now on the right, to reach a stile. Go over, cross a field and a lane to go through the iron, waymarked gate opposite. Go along the field to reach a sandy 'gallop' (for racehorses). Take this for a few yards to reach a gate. Go through and head left across fields and stiles, staying close to woodland to reach a gate on to a drive. Go along this, passing a white cottage to reach a lane. Turn left. Follow the lane past a barn and turn left at the first walkway sign, by a large dwelling set back. Bear slightly right to go cross a waymarked stile, continuing to the trig point on Hob Hill. Just beyond there are good views of the snaking M42, the Lickey Hills and the jutting Frankley Beeches. To the left is Redditch.

Ahead, and downhill, is a stile: go over on to a lane, cross and follow the waymark sign opposite. Go through farm outbuildings on a broad track, following it to reach an iron gate on to a lane. Turn right for a few yards, then go over a stile on the left. Cross a wooden bridge and bear right uphill to reach a stile. Go over and cross a field to reach another stile between trees. Go over and walk around the perimeter of **Seachem Farm** to pick up a bridleway. Follow this past large outbuildings to reach a lane. Turn right for 200 yards, then go left on the signed bridleway which leads past Lodge Farm to reach the outward route. Now retrace your steps back into Alvechurch.

POINTS OF INTEREST:
Seachem Farm - This farm has an exquisite 14th-century half-timbered section.

REFRESHMENTS:
Nothing on the walk, but there is a choice in Alvechurch.

Walk 79   **FROMES HILL AND BOSBURY**   7^1/$_2$m (12km)

Maps: OS Sheets Landranger 149; Pathfinder 1018.

Good countryside, but some difficult, undefined rights of way.

Start: At 681465, the Wheatsheaf Inn, Fromes Hill.

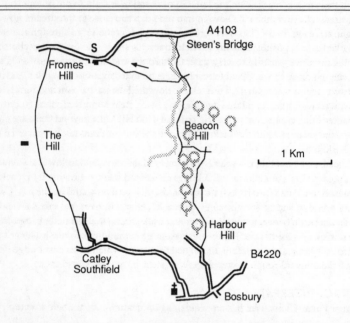

Go west along the A4103, with great care, for nearly ^{1}/$_2$ mile to reach, on the right, two detached houses very close together. Opposite, that is on the left, is a walking sign. Follow the indicated route across a field, possibly cropped in summer. About 100 yards right of a line of trees there is a stile in a hedge. Go over and keep to the right around the next field to reach an iron gate. Go through, turn right, then left and near the end of the field look to the right for a stile and iron gate. Go over and turn left along the hop field beyond. Go right and left at the next iron gate so that the hedge is on now on your left. Go over stiles each end of a plank over a ditch and head for a solitary oak which stands about 100 yards to the left of the farm buildings on the right. In the next field there are fine views towards May Hill, Oyster Hill and the Malverns. Pass close to an old rusty barn in the adjacent field, to the right, and go

152

through a gap/old gate. Follow the fence dividing the fields and go right over a stile. Go down to reach groups of trees and hug the left-hand side of a thicket to reach a wooden bridge on the left. Beyond this go right along the stream bank, which is guarded by a thicket. Go through two gates to reach a black and white timbered house. Turn left along the drive to reach a lane. Go right along the lane to a T-junction. Turn left towards a telephone box. Now ignore the temptation to turn right into a drive which apparently leads to rights of way to Bosbury. There is no trace of these, so stay on this very pleasant lane all the way to **Bosbury**.

Walk east out of Bosbury leaving the B4220 along the first lane to the left. Walk past several houses to reach the first major drive, to the right. It is signed 'No Through Road' and 'Private' and for Kynance Stud, Noverings Farm etc. At the last building along the drive, go through two iron gates on to a green track. This runs along field bottoms, going through several gates. About $\frac{1}{2}$ mile or so after the last farm, and just before coming level with an isolated house on the far right, look carefully up towards the woods to find a stile. Go over into the woods and go immediately right before twisting left to reach a cross-ways. Go straight over and walk down a muddy, vehicular track to emerge in a clearing by cut wood stacks. Go through a gate and turn right on to a good track. This can now be followed all the way to the main A4103. There, turn left and follow the road with great care back to the starting inn. A good alternative, but one not easy to locate, is to take a poorly defined path, to the left, on a bend about 1000 yards along the track. The path improves, following field edges and passing close to two buildings (a farm and a detached, red house) before reaching a lane. Follow the lane to the A4103 and turn left, with care, to return to the Wheatsheaf Inn.

POINTS OF INTEREST:
Bosbury - The Church of the Holy Trinity has a chantry chapel and a detached bell tower, one of seven in Herefordshire. Between the years 1230 and 1240 the church was often used as refuge by local folk escaping armed incursions by the Welsh.

REFRESHMENTS:
The Wheatsheaf Inn, Fromes Hill.
The Bell Inn, Bosbury.

Walk 80 KNIGHTWICK AND MARTLEY 7¹/₂m (12km)

Maps: OS Sheets Landranger 150; Pathfinder 995.
A fine example of Worcestershire countryside.
Start: At 734560, the Talbot Inn, Knightwick.

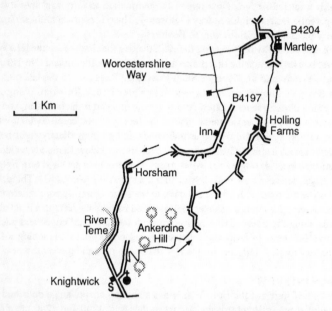

Walk towards the church, continuing up the hill along the B4197. Turn right at a footpath sign and ascend quite steeply through woods, zig-zagging along the waymarked Worcestershire Way. Pass a garage and fenced enclosure, then turn left around a property. Go past a niche, to the left, where there are a bench and picnic table, continuing to reach Willow Cottage. Turn right beside its garage on a path down the edge of a wood with a field to the left. Cross a stile by a barn and go down a field. Bear right towards the boundary fence to reach two gates in the corner. Go through the gate into a wood and, after 30 yards, turn left along an uphill track to reach a Worcestershire Way post. Turn right to reach a T-junction (and another waymarker post). Turn right again. Turn left at the next post to reach a gate and, beyond, a steep field. Trend right and up towards woodland and follow its edge, going through two gates to reach a lane. Turn left. Go past a farm to reach a waymarked junction. Bear right along a lane and go over a signed stile, to the right. Keep near to the cables and go into the next field. Go over a stile and cross the lane beyond to another. Keep to the hedge of the field beyond to reach a Worcestershire Way sign at the bottom. Kink left, then right through a gap and go up a field to a gate. Go through and turn left along a lane to reach a cross-roads. Go straight over (signed Martley). Go through Holling Farms, continuing to reach a walkway sign to the right. Cross an orchard by way of two stiles. **Martley Church** is seen ahead now and there are also good views of Woodbury and Abberley Hills. Stiles at each end of a plank lead to a field. Follow its left edge, then go right on a path ahead heading towards the church. Leave the field on to a lane, walking ahead to reach the church drive. Go through the yard to reach the B4204 and turn left into the village. The Crown Inn is at the junction.

From the inn go right with the road passing the Memorial Hall and playing fields, to the left. On a sharp left bend go straight ahead along a 'No Through Road' signed for Kingswood. After a few hundred yards, opposite a sharp right bend, go left on the Worcestershire Way, heading south to reach a house on a lane. Kink left and right (waymarked) to pick up a track. Cross two stiles and two fields to reach a white cottage with stile by its corner. Go over and follow a drive to a road (the B4197). Turn right passing the Admiral Rodney Inn. Continue along the road, then bear right, off it, towards Horsham. Descend to a white gate signed 'The Old Forge'. Next to it, cross a stile/plank and descend into a shallow valley, trending left to cross a plank to reach a hedge gap. Continue towards trees beyond which there is a gate into a rough field. Follow the right border, but ignoring a stile in it. Walk to a fence jump and gate and cross the field beyond to a farm. Go over a stile into the yard. Turn right, then left through a gate on to a drive passing an ivy-decked building, left. The drive picks up the River Teme which is followed for a short stretch. Go through a large farm and follow the drive, which becomes metalled, back into Knightwick.

POINTS OF INTEREST:

Martley Church - The bell tower has the oldest complete ring of six bells in England, cast by Richard Keene of Woodstock in 1673. There is also a fine wooden screen an effigy of Sir Hugh Mortimer, Lord of Martley and Kyre who was killed at the Battle of Wakefield in 1459.

REFRESHMENTS:

The Crown Inn, Martley.
Admiral Rodney Inn, on the B4197.
The Talbot Inn, Knightwick.

Walk 81 RICHARDS CASTLE AND HIGH VINNALS $7^1/_2$m (12km)

Maps: OS Sheets Landranger 137; Pathfinder 972.
A fine walk in the delectable north Herefordshire countryside.
Start: At 493697, in Richards Castle.

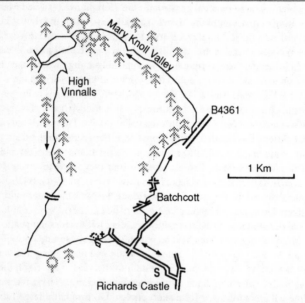

Head north-west along the lane out of the village to reach a cross-roads. Go over
(signed Goggin, Elton and Ludlow). Turn right and walk to the last house on the left,
which lies far back up a drive. Just beyond this there is a stile to the left. Go over and
follow the right-hand edge of a field to reach a track that leads to a lane. Turn right.
Just beyond a small green drive by ash trees there is a hidden stile on the left. Go over
and turn right immediately to cross two fields linked by a gap. Continue on a track
through a gate by a house on the left. Go through another gate to reach a cross-ways.
Go straight ahead past a property, to the right, where a wide track curves round from
left to right. Now head north-eastwards, passing two cottages and crossing into
Shropshire. Go over a cross-ways, continuing through bracken and mixed woodland.
Bear slightly right and descend, ignoring a track to the left, to go over a stile by a
pond. Go over a stile to reach the B4361 opposite the entrance to Moor Park School.

Turn left for 250 yards to reach a large forestry road on the left. In the far corner there is a track entering the wood: take this, swinging left, but do not trend uphill. Instead, look carefully for a track to the right which descends to reach a broader one. Turn left to meet another wide track into Sunny Dingle (signed). Bear right at a fork to reach a three way fork. Take the path marked by a post to emerge on the main forestry road again, gradually rising up Mary Knoll Valley. Ignore a left branch by a fir-lined valley continuing to a post at a cross-roads. There is a welcome bench a few yards to the right. Turn right, then bend left to reach a post with several colour bands. Cross a wider track, which has a red and green striped post, taking the track opposite. Ascend this steeply to reach a red striped post. Now go steeply right up to the summit of **High Vinnals**, crowned by a wooden watch tower.

Descend the track ahead to a T-junction. Turn left and, almost immediately, right at a post to skirt the forest to reach a gate into a field. Follow the right-hand hedge to reach a metalled lane. Cross and continue on a track, still with a hedge to the right. Bear rightwards away from a gate, then veer left to an elongated corner of the field where a gate leads to a track between hedges. Follow the track to reach two gates on opposite sides. Go through the left gate and go along the left hedge towards a tree-topped hill. Go through a gate at the corner of the trees to reach two tracks. Take the left, lower, track. Cross a ford and note, up on the left, an old church with a detached bell tower. Keep to the left of some farm buildings to reach a lane. Here go left, uphill, if you wish to visit the St Bartholomew's Church, Richards Castle. Otherwise turn right to reach the outward route and follow this back to the start.

POINTS OF INTEREST:
High Vinnals - On clear days the view from here includes the Black Mountains, Brecon Beacons, Radnor Forest, the Arans, Corndon Hill, the Stiperstones, the Long Mynd, Ragleth Hill, the Wrekin, the Clees, Clent Hills, Abberley Hills, the tip of Bredon Hill, the Cotswolds and the Malverns.

REFRESHMENTS:
None on the walk, but there is a fine choice in Ludlow.

Walk 82   OLD STORRIDGE COMMON & ALFRICK   7¹/₂m (12km)

Maps: OS Sheets Landranger 150; Pathfinder 995.

Wooded hills and dales make a fine first section.

Start: At 760494, the New Inn on the A4104.

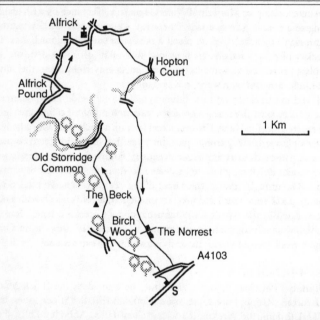

About 20 yards north of the Inn is the Worcestershire Way. Turn left along a field hedge, go through a gap and cross a track. Go past a waymarker post and over a stile into an orchard. Be cautious at the next post, which offers a confusing signal. Keep your line, passing between two holly trees to reach another post. Bear left, uphill, on a track into a wood, then follow waymarkers through more orchards to reach a gate. Turn right, then left to go over stiles, around a cottage, on to a lane. Turn right and in a few yards bear right up a drive for 'Birchwood Hall, Anybody's Barn'. Leave the drive on a track to the right, passing a house, left, through its gardens and orchard. Bear right to an oak tree and a stile. Go over and turn left. Go over a stile 50 yards right of the left corner of the field and follow a track down into woodland to reach an angled lane junction. Turn sharp left, pass two cottages and take a broad track bearing right. Cross a footbridge to reach a sign for Knapp and Paper Mill. Go through a gate, follow a field edge by a cottage and then meander close to the Leigh Brook to reach a stile. Go through a gate and cross a field aiming just right of the houses ahead. Go through a gate and turn right along a lane. Go through the first gate to the left. Go diagonally left and through the left-hand of two gates. Follow the hedge on your right to reach a gate in a corner. Go right, then left to reach a gate on to a lane. Turn right to a junction and go left to a cross-roads. Turn right. At the next T-junction turn left into Alfrick, passing the **church** to reach a cross-roads and the village cross. Turn right to reach the Swan Inn.

From the Swan Inn, turn left and walk to a metalled drive on the right. Take this to a house, left, rounding it on a grassed way on the right by the wall. Just before a gate, kink left and go over a stile on the right. Go along a hedge, right, to reach a gap beyond a solitary post. Veer right down by two shacks, go over rough ground and follow trees by a stream, bearing right. Cross a footbridge, a field and a stile. Cross the next field to rejoin the stream. Cross this by bridge passing a thatched cottage to reach a lane. Turn left, then first right along a drive, passing a white cottage. Now follow a green track keeping left when two tracks are met. Look carefully for a gap, left, after a few yards, go through and turn right along a field. Go over the car park of a house and up a bank to turn left along a track. Cross two fields and then go through a gap in a hedge. Hug a field edge, with an orchard, right, to find a lonely house. Take the track on its left and continue on a drive past modern homes (The Norrest) to arrive at a bungalow/off licence. Turn right and take the first track to the left to return to the New Inn.

POINTS OF INTEREST:
Alfrick Church - Be sure to see the sundial with its motto 'On this moment hangs eternity' on the unique timber framed belfry tower.

REFRESHMENTS:
The Swan Inn, Alfrick.
The New Inn, at the start.

Walk 83   KINGSFORD COUNTRY PARK   7¹/₂m (12km)

Maps: OS Sheets Landranger 138; Pathfinder 932.

A walk that improves all the way round.

Start: At 831811, on the grass verge.

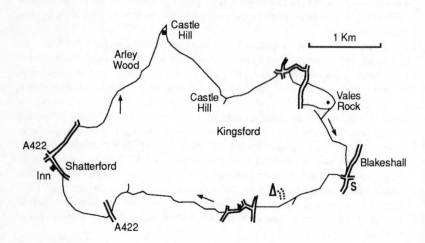

Walk east for 60 yards to the cross-roads. Turn left and follow a lane as it swings left to reach a corner and a sign 'Dead End except Footpath'. Take the path, passing Moat Court Farm, right, and Solcum Stud, left. Go to the right of a white house and over a stile (sign for Kingsford Lane). Descend a mini ravine and, beyond, note the **cliff dwellings** above and right. Cross a road (Slad Lane - Worcestershire Way) with a telephone box, left. Go into a caravan site and follow the road to reach a gate. Turn left and, in a few yards, go right over a stile. A field path leads uphill to a stile: go over, swap sides of the trees and climb to a stile. Turn right through a gap/stile and go steeply uphill and left to reach a stile by a black gate. From here there is a superb view of Kingsford Country Park. The walk levels out to reach a gate/stile. Follow a drive to the left, passing a wildlife sanctuary and pool, to reach the A442. Cross, with care, and follow a lane round to meet the A442 again. Turn left to reach the Bellman's

Cross Inn. Cross the road and turn sharp right down a lane. Bear right on a bridleway by a red-brick cottage, passing Underhill Farm before swinging left into a wood. Do not go around a hairpin bend: instead, go straight on, ignoring, too, a track going right to follow the left fence, near the woodland edge. Descend to a stream at a corner and go right to reach a T-junction with a forestry track. Turn left and follow the track under pylon lines, passing a gate, right, to reach an entrance to Start's Green Farm (a gate on the right). To the right of this, turn sharp right along a track beside the farm to reach a sign for 'Castle Hill Farm'. Continue along the track, kinking diagonally right and looking for the path signs, one of which is fixed to a tree. The track reaches a gate, with stiles to the right and left. Go over the left stile, walk over a rise and dip sharply down with a tree lined valley to the left to reach a stile in the bottom corner. Cross a small stream and bear left, then back right to keep the stream a few yards to the right. Go over a stile and follow a field edge to reach a railing stile into a lane. Turn right, then go over at a cross-roads, passing 'Birds Barn Cottage', and turn sharp right by a brick farm building. Go round a property, left, and a paddock, right, to reach a lane. Turn right and go over a rise to reach the entrance, left, to Kingsford Country Park. A broad path leads through birch trees to the base of the imposing Vales Rock with more cliff dwellings. Climb up the Rock (narrow and precipitous, but exciting and safe for steady heads - an easier option goes straight on along the Worcestershire Way). Switch back left and climb steeply to the ridge and walk to its edge. Turn right, then bear left by a waymarker post. Go round left of a reservoir, kink left and right at the next post. Take one of two parallel paths. Turn left at the T-junction and right by wooden gates to pass a red-brick house and a bungalow, above and right. Bear right on to a lane to return to the start.

POINTS OF INTEREST:

Cliff dwellings - These dwellings in the sandstone cliff were only abandoned 40-50 years ago.

REFRESHMENTS:

The Bellman's Cross Inn, on the route.

Walk 84   WIGMORE AND LINGEN   8m (13km)

Maps: OS Sheets Landranger 148; Pathfinder 971 and 972.

A beautiful corner of Herefordshire, wooded hills and dales.

Start: At 415691, in Wigmore.

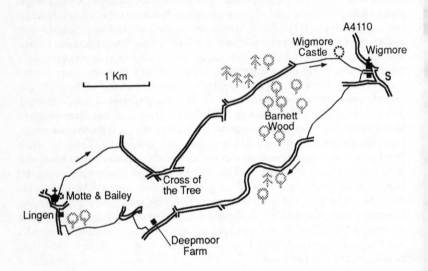

Go along the A4110, and take a bridleway opposite the post office. Just beyond a wood carvers', left, go right through a gate and bear left up a hedge/gully. Go over a waymarked stile and then another on to a lane. Turn right for 70 yards, then go left over a stile. Go diagonally right to the bottom left corner of a field. Go over a stile and a ditch and turn right through a field to reach a stile into another. At its upper end take the right-hand of two gates and go along the edge of a fenced copse, left, to reach a gate on the left. Bear left to a gate and go left of an arm of trees to reach a stile on to a lane. Bear right along the wooded lane for $^1/_2$ mile to where it dips down to cross a stream. Turn left along a green track for another $^1/_2$ mile to reach a lane at a bend. Go ahead, uphill, to where the lane swings right at a triangle of grass. Ignore a track, left, maintaining direction on a drive which splits at a farm gate. Keep ahead on a green ride to where, opposite two gates, a track goes right. Where this swings left to a barn, take the green track branching right. Beyond a gate this, too, splits: keep ahead but just before a field, go through a gate, left, and swing right into a dip. Go through a gate and cross a log bridge over a stream to meet a track. Go left and at a very sharp right bend, go left through a gate and cross a field towards a domed tree-covered hill on the horizon. Go through a gap and follow the track to the left of trees and over the crest. Go down to a stile into a plantation. Swing downhill and left to the bottom, then go right along the base to reach two bridges. Cross to a third bridge and a stile on the right. Go over and turn left, crossing the stream again to reach a gate into Lingen. Turn right to reach the Royal George. From it, go towards the church, going through the lych gate and yard. Go along the left side and over a stile into a field where there are the remains of a motte and bailey. Go over the bridge ahead and cross a field to reach a gate/stile. Turn right to go through another gate and walk to a stream. Turn left and follow it. Turn right over a bridge and cross the stile beyond. Go left to reach a bridge and stile. Follow the left edge of the next field towards a green knoll. Go over two stiles to reach the foot of the knoll, bearing left of it to cross a stile on to a lane. Turn right, then left at the cross-roads (signed Dickendale and Wigmore). Turn left along a lane which becomes a track, following it to a lane. Turn left and follow the lane through a forest. About 200 yards beyond a steep ascent there is a stile to the left: go over and walk around the right edge to a stile. Cross a field towards **Wigmore Castle** going over a stile on to a fenced track along its base. Take a parallel thin path adjacent to the track, going through gates on to drive which is followed back into Wigmore.

POINTS OF INTEREST:
Wigmore Castle - Once the seat of the Mortimer family and rebuilt in the 14th century by Roger Mortimer. He was the Queen's lover, was involved in the murder of Edward II and was executed. The castle was dismantled to avoid damage in the Civil War.

REFRESHMENTS:
The Royal George, Lingen.
The Old Oak Inn, Wigmore.
The Compasses Inn, Wigmore.

Walk 85 MAMBLE, MENITHWOOD AND LINDRIDGE 8m (13km)

Maps: OS Sheets Landranger 138; Pathfinder 952 and 973.
Undulating fields and woods. Tricky route finding in one wood.
Start: At 692715, by the village hall in Mamble.

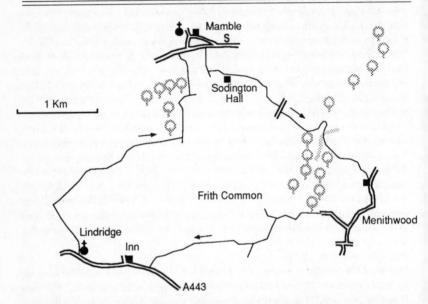

Go east along the village lane to the A456 and turn right, with care, along it. After a short distance turn left into a lane, ignoring a field path on the left corner. Opposite an open space and a barn, to the right, go over a waymarked stile and cross a field, passing a pond, to reach another stile. Now ignore a stile on the far right and carry straight on past a second pond. Just before an iron gate, go over a stile on the right and turn left. Go through a gap and turn right along a track over a brow to reach a gap by a holly tree. Turn left by an ash tree, going along a wide track to reach a gate on to a lane. Cross and go down a gated drive to a timber company. Go through a pleasant avenue of trees, and where the metalled drive turns sharp left, leave it for a green track on the right. After 100 yards the track splits: bear left on a woodland track, descending and swinging right by a tiny bench. Continue, passing paths to the left and right. There is a footbridge down to the right: ignore this, bearing left on a path that

164

reaches a thickly wooded bottom where two small streams meet. You must cross the stream here. It looks as though there is no way ahead, but it is a right of way. Go through a few yards of undergrowth and over a low barbed wire fence. Now go up and right across a field to reach a gate. Beyond, dip down, noting, far left at the top, Stildon Manor. Aim for its left side going through gates and the yard/drive to reach a lane. Turn right and follow the lane into Menithwood. Walk through the village and turn right along a 'No Through Road'. At its end, take a bridleway into a wood. Emerge at a bridge and turn right towards a white cottage. Swing left on a gated lane to reach a sawmill and bear right on a path through a gate. Go along a hedge, kinking right and left to reach a gate, by pylons to the right, into a wood. Follow the woodland path to reach a gate. Go through, cross a field and go through another gate into an orchard. Continue along a metalled drive, passing a couple of houses and a pond, to reach the A443. Turn right, with care, to reach Lindridge and the Nag's Head Inn.

From the inn, go along the main road to the church, taking a path on its left side through the cemetery to reach a gate into a field. Bear left to go up over a brow to reach a stile into an orchard. Go down its left edge through a gap/stile to reach a drive. Go diagonally right across this and over two stiles and an orchard to reach a stile by a large red-brick house. Cross its drive and a stile into a field. Cross this and a stile on to a track. Turn left and immediately right through a gate. Follow the boundary fence, passing a cottage and going through a gate on to a track. Branch right on a green track within an orchard boundary to reach a gate/stile. Cross two fields going uphill and aiming for pylons. Keep a woodland edge 60 yards to the left, then go acutely under the pylon lines and through a gate between two hawthorns. Go through a gate under smaller cables and cross a waymarked stile on the left. Go over and turn right. Go through a waymarked gate, but ignore another to the right. Turn left at the end boundary and, after 80 yards, go right over a waymarked stile. Cross scrub to another stile. Go over and turn left to reach a gate to the left of a waymarked post. About 100 yards beyond, go left over a stile and cross towards a boundary. Skirt a lake and take the left-hand of two ways at the next gate. Follow a woodland edge to reach a stile into trees. Pass a new pond, and go through two gates and over a stile near stables to reach the A456. Turn right, then left to return to the start in Mamble.

REFRESHMENTS:
The Nag's Head, Lindridge.

Walk 86   GOODRICH AND COPPET HILL   8½ m (13½ km)

Maps: OS Sheets Landranger 162; Outdoor Leisure 14.
Following the beautiful Wye Valley, then a cracking hill to finish.
Start: At 575193, the Post Office, Goodrich village.

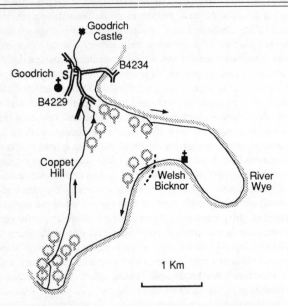

Go along the 'No Through Road' to Welsh Bicknor. Where this crosses over the B4228 there is a stile in the wall. Go over and down to the B road, following it downhill with a glimpse of **Goodrich Castle** far left (the castle can be visited at the start or end of the walk, adding ¾ mile to the walk distance). Continue to a five-arched bridge over the River Wye and join the Wye Valley Walk, to the right. Cross two stiles and two fields to reach a woodland river section where steps reach a higher level. Cross the bottom of a garden of a stone cottage continuing past a pointless stile. Traverse a jungle of Himalayan Balsam laced with nettles (even in summer!) to enter woodland once more. Finally, and with relief, go over a stile into a meadow. Cross to a gate with track rising right into woodland. Do not take this: instead, go over a waymarked stile and take the green riverside path, crossing another stile. Go around a long right-hand bend. to see, ahead, Welsh Bicknor Church and Youth Hostel. Take a high route by

166

the hostel or a low route close to the river, the two routes eventually meeting again. Go under an old railway bridge and cross some tangled roots to reach a good path which goes through dense thickets into a meadow. Go through a gate into bracken noting, ahead and on the opposite bank, Coldwell Rocks, a protected nesting site for peregrine falcons. Cross a series of meadows, further woodland and more meadows as you bend around beneath Coldwell Rocks with Yat Rock conspicuous at the far end of the bend. A stile by a willow is signed two ways: it is possible to continue straight ahead, following the river to reach a lane and then the B road back to Goodrich.

However, a much finer finale is to take the signed path up Coppet Hill. So turn right and, shortly, enter a wood over a stile. This does not appear to be a right of way, but it is waymarked and concessionary. Climb up a track through thick wood to reach an area of bracken with occasional views out across the valley. Follow a drystone wall under low trees, the view really opening out leftwards over the tremendous bend on the Wye as it virtually U-turns at Symonds Yat, both East and West villages being well seen. Beyond are Garway Hill and the Black Mountains. Near at hand, in early autumn, there is a blackberry pickers' paradise! Continue for some distance in this fine elevated position dipping slightly before ascending to the highest part of the hill by a line of trees on the right, ignoring any tracks downhill left. Note Goodrich and the castle far below, then bear left for a few yards to reach the trig. point, which is some yards downhill. Note the road bridge far down on the right and look across to see Abergavenny Sugar Loaf, part of Ysgyryd Fawr and, through the gap beyond, the Brecon Beacons. Penyard Hill and Ross-on-Wye are prominent ahead. Descend steeply to reach steps, with waymarked posts to the left. Kink left, then right to pass a large sandstone boulder and then zig-zag down further steps to reach a lane which is taken left back into Goodrich.

POINTS OF INTEREST:
Goodrich Castle - This early 12th century castle is the best preserved in Herefordshire. It is mostly of local red sandstone, though the Norman keep is grey. It is now owned by English Heritage and is the scene of Mediaeval entertainment at peak summer times.

REFRESHMENTS:
The Post Office/Stores in Goodrich and the snack-bar at the Castle car park.

Walk 87   KINGTON AND RUSHOCK HILL   8½m (13½km)

Maps: OS Sheets Landranger 148; Pathfinder 993 and 971.

A recommended route through the Welsh Marches.

Start: At 296566, the Tourist Information Centre, Kington.

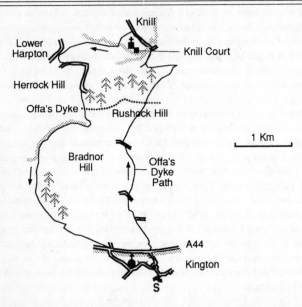

There is a car park beside the Centre. Turn right from it, passing toilets and turning sharp left to The Square. Turn right, noting an Offa's Dyke Path waymarker. Kink around cottages and cross a bridge over a tributary of the River Arrow. Cross the town bypass and follow Offa's Dyke Path up a little lane, ignoring a stile, right, to go through a waymarked gate. Follow a hedged track, then go up a field, going through kissing gates at each end. Another hedged track leads past three houses to reach two more near a waymarked post. Now simply follow the posts uphill and admire the views over Kington, the Black Mountains and Brecon Beacons. Go up a shallow trough through a golf course to reach a road and, almost immediately, turn right over a cattle grid. Go left along a wall and through a gate with a clump of trees ahead. There is a red-tiled building, sharp right: steer away from this up the left-hand hedge to reach a stile at the edge of some trees. Go over and follow a track beside a fence.

168

The thinner track beyond reaches a stile. Go over this and another a few yards beyond, and then head for the corner of a plantation. Bear left to reach the next stile and cross Rushock Hill aiming for a skyline mast. Just before the mast the prominent Offa's Dyke Path crosses, at a gate. Ignore it, going through the gate and bearing right to a waymarked stile. Take a middle course down the field beyond, with the attractive Hindwell Brook Valley stretched out ahead and the Clees beyond, to reach a waymarked gate. Go ahead for a few yards, then turn right along a green track. After 20 yards follow a yellow arrow down into the woods to the left. Switchback on the first bend of a track which could well be overgrown, cross a forest track and follow an improving path to meet a signed forestry track going right. Take this down to a ford near cottages. Cross a bridge over Hindwell Brook and follow a lane towards Knill, a fine half-timbered farm. At this point it is worth a diversion left to inspect Knill Church.

At the end of a corrugated barn of Knill Farm, go left through a gate and up a field to reach another. Now go down and left, going around a house to reach a stile into its grounds. There, an ornate bridge crosses the stream. It **is** the Right of Way despite the 'Private' sign. Go over a stile into a field and bear right with a stream. This field can be muddy when wet but there is compensation in the fine surrounding country, with the prominent Whimble on Radnor Forest ahead. Go through a gate into an even longer field, leaving the main stream to follow a tributary. Cross another large field to reach farm buildings and Offa's Dyke Path. Go left with a hedge to reach a gate on to a lane. Go left to pass a cottage, then continue on a track which veers rightwards around a hill. Now take an uphill, slanting track over a col and head straight down beyond a three waymarked sign, ignoring Offa's Dyke Path, to the left. Go straight down through a gate in a corner and go left to cross a prominent stile. Go right, over a stream, and follow its bank down a valley. About 100 yards from some farm buildings, bear left to pass a waymarked post. Go over a stile and follow a track as it contours around to a wood. Go in, and turn left, uphill, on a track through a gap in the firs. Where the track splits, keep on the level to reach a path (signed with a 'foot'). Go uphill along the woodland edge for 100 yards, then go right at another 'foot' sign to reach a gate. Go through and follow a lane at the end of the trees. Go past a cottage and turn right, then left before a cattle grid. Contour a hill, passing a newish cottage. Cross a waymarked stile beyond, and go downhill to reach another. Keep descending, going through a gate at the bottom on to a track which heads towards Kington church spire. Go past a barn to reach the main A44. Cross, with care, and go up a lane to the church and, from it, back into Kington.

REFRESHMENTS:

There are numerous possibilities in Kington.

Walk 88   ROSS-ON-WYE AND PENYARD PARK $8\frac{1}{2}$m ($13\frac{1}{2}$km)

Maps: OS Sheets Landranger 162; Pathfinder 1065.

An historic town and three wooded hills make a fine walk.

Start: At 598244, the long stay car park, Ross-on-Wye.

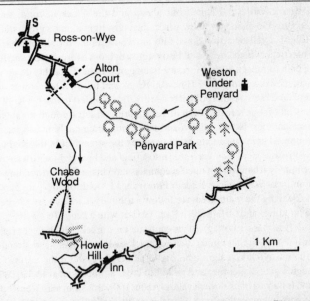

Walk to **St Mary's Church** and, from the churchyard, go past the Plague Cross and turn left into Church Street. Turn right at the bottom, passing the 17th-century Market Cross. Turn right along the B4228 and left into Alton Street. Turn right into Merrivale Lane leaving it by a small green to go over a signed stile into a field. Aim for the wood ahead, entering it through a gate. Turn right and walk to steps going up on the left. Climb these to emerge on to a lateral track. Turn right through a kissing gate with a Wye Valley Walk sign. Go past large buildings, left, and take the left-hand of two ways towards a forestry bar across the route. You are now on the Wye Valley Walk. Follow it into thick woodland, descending a surprisingly long and steep route, occasionally stepped, to reach the valley. Go through gates and fields to reach a lane. Go left to reach the next waymarked stile, to the right. Climb up, cross a drive by the gates of Craig Farmo and go up again through trees to reach a cottage. Turn right and follow its drive to a T-Junction. Ignore the arrow pointing right, downhill, and go up a part-metalled, curving drive to reach a T-junction. Turn left and walk to the next junction. Bear left to reach a sign for the Crown Inn, down a steep drive to the left. Go left from the Crown Inn, passing the St James' Church. Turn right by 'Wooleys' and walk to a signpost. Take the thinner of two paths down a hedged gully, cross a track (yellow waymark on a tree) and descend to reach a lane. Turn left and almost immediately right, opposite a cottage. Leave this drive over a stile, right, into a field, bypassing the cottage ahead. Cross the next field to reach a stile into a wood. Cross a path and go up a wooded gully, crossing another path above. Go over a stile into a field. Follow its edge to reach a gap and turn left on a drive. Pass a cottage, left, and when another cottage is reached, go right of it down a path through trees to join a drive from another house on the left. Go round left at the bottom to reach a lane. Turn right, passing the Dayla Soft Drinks factory. Stay with the lane and about 100 yards past an isolated post box, turn left on to a drive. Curve around behind some cottages to reach a thin path going uphill towards woods. Follow the edge of the woods to meet a track. Veer left to reach a junction of three ways. Go left, uphill, and swing right at the top to pass farm buildings. Go over stiles and gates to reach a woodland edge behind a wire fence. Go through thicker woodland to reach a wide forestry track. Bear right on this until it begins a curve right. There, go left over a stile into a field. Look for a waymarked oak and turn sharp right, downhill, on a path to reach a fenced wood and waymarked post. Cross two stiles and turn left down a steep field. Go through a kissing gate and turn left along a path, passing the timbered Alton Court. Turn left into Alton Street and retrace your steps back to the start.

POINTS OF INTEREST:
St Mary's Church, Ross - The creepers in the church replace two trees dedicated to John Kyrle 1637-1724, 'The Man of Ross', a benefactor of the town whose monument is near the altar. The Plague Cross commemorates 315 victims who died 1637.

REFRESHMENTS:
The Crown Inn, Howle Hill.
There are also numerous choices in Ross.

Walk 89 BROMYARD AND THE FROME VALLEY 8½m (13½km)

Maps: OS Sheets Landranger 149; Pathfinder 995.

Early route finding leads to undulating walking.

Start: At 653548, the Conquest Theatre car park, Bromyard.

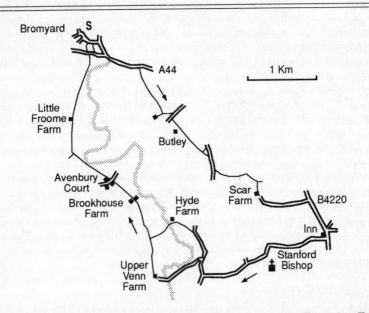

From the Theatre go back towards the town and turn left to reach a T-junction. Turn right to reach Shepford Street and right again by the Crown and Sceptre Inn to descend to the main A44. Turn left along the pavement, passing **Linton Pound**, a walled enclosure. Continue towards a large farm on the left. Just before and opposite are two gates: go through either and cross a field to a line of four trees. Beyond these, go slightly left to a solitary tree and then downhill and through a hedge gap. Turn right up a field going by way of a strange contraption to a field beyond. Follow the right edge to reach a stile. Go over and turn left down a track, by Lodor Farm, to reach a T-junction. Turn sharp right up a lane. A footpath sign points left: follow this across a strip of land to reach a waymarked stile. Bear right to a line of trees and then go slightly left across a field to another waymarked stile. Go over two further stiles and under electricity cables. Go over a stile, cross a farm track and over another stile. Go

172

left over the next stile, hidden by a tree, on to a lane. Take the signed path opposite going downhill and right to reach two stiles in a hedge. Go over and turn sharp left, downhill, with a holly hedge to the left. Go over another stile at the bottom and cross a field aiming for the right side of a cottage where there is a stile. Go over and either cross a bridge or a covered culvert and go steeply uphill to Scar Farm. Go left of the farm on a track which leads to the B4220. Turn right and walk to the Herefordshire House Inn. Continue along the road, then turn right on a road to Stanford Bishop Church. To reach the church - from where there are extensive views to Bromyard Downs, the Malverns, the Suckley Hills and across the graceful Frome Valley - you must divert left.

Continue along the road but, at the bottom of the hill, turn right at a T-junction. Leave the road by turning left at a signed gate to Upper Venn Farm. Go through the buildings and walk straight ahead to a gate. Cross a tiny stream and the field beyond to reach a line of trees. Follow the track, now hard-cored, through Brookhouse Farm. Ignore tracks to the right and left and go over the stile ahead. Cross a field towards the prominent Avenbury Court. Go over a stile and a bridge, going along the edge of a hopyard. Go through a gate and cross a field to reach another close to the Court. Cross a lane to another (signed) gate, trend left over the next field to reach a stile. Beyond, walk parallel to the River Frome. Cross a stream by way of a plank and go over a slight rise to reach a gate in a corner. Continue along a well marked green track, passing (the big) Little Froome Farm. Continue towards the A44, noting the timber-framed **Tower House**. Take the underpass beneath the main road to reach Pump Street, Bromyard. Now take the short journey back to the car park.

POINTS OF INTEREST:
Linton Pound – This is an ancient stray animal pen.
Tower House – Charles I stayed here in 1644.

REFRESHMENTS:
The Herefordshire House Inn, on the route.
There are also choices in Bromyard.

Walk 90 ABBERLEY HILL AND WOODBURY HILL $8^1/_2$m ($13^1/_2$km)

Maps: OS Sheets Landranger 138; Pathfinder 973.

Up and down over wooded hills with occasional excellent views.

Start: At 753662, the Hundred House Inn at Great Witley.

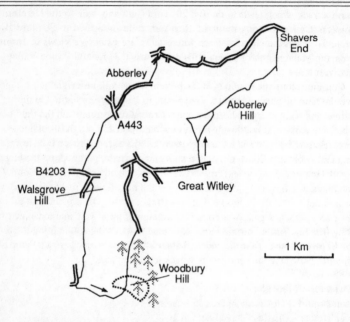

Walk east along the pavement beside the A451 and turn left at a bridleway to Shavers End. Walk steadily uphill and fork right at a bridleway sign. The way can be overgrown: go through the bracken, nettles and brambles to reach a Worcestershire Way post and another just beyond. The path becomes easier and levels out: bear right on the Worcestershire Way, then kink right and left to reach a T-junction. Here a brief diversion left reaches an excellent viewpoint. The route now goes right, descending with the Worcestershire Way. Turn left and emerge from the trees to bear left across a field. Go through a gap in the trees and turn left. Go under small pylons and turn left on to a lane. Follow the lane into Abberley.

Be sure to visit **St Michael's Church** then go across the village square to reach a path signed Wynniats Way. Follow a drive for a few yards, then turn left along a

field edge and go over a stile. Turn right, u[...]
edge of a wood. Go steeply through the woo[...]
a Worcestershire Way sign and carry on dov[...]
care, and follow a bridleway beside a deer pa[...]
to reach the B4203. Turn left and pass some[...]
Lane. After 70 yards go left over a stile into a[...]
the Worcestershire Way down and right throug[...]
path sign. Go over on to a lane and turn left[...]
through red gates. Climb up through woods to[...]
ahead, bearing left through a hedge gap. Follov[...]
left, and going through an old gate. Now, at t[...]
choice of routes. Either go ahead towards a large [...] back left, or climb
immediately left, and steeply, to reach a path an[...] turn right. Shortly, turn left on a
wider path – reached from the opposite direction by the first choice. Woodbury Hill is
covered in trees so its earthworks are hidden. Go down the wider path and where it
swings left, bear right. Next, where the track goes right, bear right on a thin path down
to a lane. Turn left and follow the lane to its junction with the B4203. Turn right to
return to the start.

POINTS OF INTEREST:
St Michael's Church, Abberley - This tiny church, partly ruined but with intact
Norman arches was built on a Saxon place of worship.

REFRESHMENTS:
The Hundred House Inn, Great Witley.
The Manor Arms, Abberley.

WHITBOURNE

$8\frac{1}{2}$m ($13\frac{1}{2}$km)
or 11m ($17\frac{1}{2}$km)

s Landranger 149; Pathfinder 995 and 973.

plifying the best of Hereford and Worcester.

/25569, Whitbourne Church.

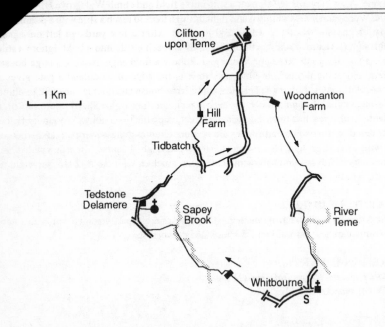

Go along the lane towards Meadow Green and bear right towards Tedstone Delamere. Follow the lane to a T-junction. On the far side is a stile: go over and follow a field edge to a gate. Go through and cross to another stile. Cross the field beyond towards some buildings. Go through a gate and over a waymarked stile on the right of the buildings. Go through an orchard to pass and follow waymarker post through another orchard to reach a track. Turn left, then right at the walking sign. Follow a hedge into a dip and turn left through a gate. Cross a field, go through a gap and cross a larger field. Cross a bridge over Sapey Brook, crossing it again to skirt below lonely Whitehall cottage to reach a stile and yet another bridge over the stream. About 50 yards beyond, turn right and first left to go steeply uphill to a T-junction. Turn right, then left to reach a lane. Turn right, soon, perhaps, bearing right to visit the isolated Church of St James, Tedstone Delamere. Continue along the lane, with Tedstone Court to the right, then turn right along a 'No Through Road'. Go downhill, passing Limehouse Farm. Ignore two tracks going right to go through a gate into a field. Descend along the right hedge to reach a gap in the corner. Drop steeply left to cross a bridge over a stream, going uphill beyond, through woods, to reach a lane.

For the shorter route, turn right, but go left through a gate at the first bend. Cross the field beyond to two gates. Go through the left one and follow a hedge to a lane. Turn left, passing Oxhall Farm to reach Saltbox, a house on the left.

For the longer route, go left along the lane. Bear right on a path (waymarked by a blue arrow) to bypass a house (Tidbatch) continuing through a wood to reach a waterfall. Turn left on a track through conifers and where this forks, go right through a gate. Go uphill along the right hedge, then veer right to reach a gate below Hill Farm. Go through the buildings and follow the long drive. Just beyond a bungalow, left, is a track which leads past an older building to a gate. Now cross fields to reach a lane into Clifton upon Teme, or follow the lane beyond the bungalow to the T-junction and turn left to Clifton.

From Clifton, take the Whitbourne road to reach Saltbox and the shorter route. Go over a concealed stile opposite the house and follow a field edge. Cross a ditch by way of stones in a gap and follow the left edge of the next field to reach Woodmanton Farm. Go through the farm, going right between the last two barns. Kink right and left over a cattle grid and follow a drive to Ayngstree, passing to its left. Continue along a field edge to reach a track descending leftwards to reach a lane. Turn right and after $1/_2$ mile go left into a field by a telegraph pole (sign). Descend rightwards through a copse to reach the River Teme. Follow the river to a pumping station and from there take a lane back into **Whitbourne**.

POINTS OF INTEREST:
Whitbourne - The present Court, near the church, is 17th century, but stands on the site of an old moated palace of the Bishop of Hereford.

REFRESHMENTS:
Nothing on the shorter route.
The Lion Inn, Clifton upon Teme, on the longer walk.

Maps: OS Sheets Landranger 149; Pathfinder 1040 and 1041.
A recommended walk for spring or early summer.
Start: At 572375, opposite the school in Mordiford.

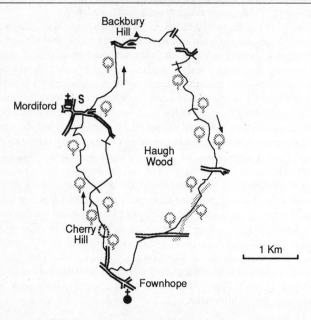

Turn left on to the B4224, leaving it immediately by a lane, to the left, passing the Moon Inn. Take the first lane left, then go left at a waymarker, going steeply through trees. Go over a stile into a field and follow the hedge to the right. Keep to the right of a hilltop copse and go over a brow to find a line of trees/hedge. Follow this to the left to reach two stiles signed 'Wye Valley Walk'. There is a ruined cottage down right and ahead a ruined barn. About 50 yards left of the barn is a stile: go over and cross a field to reach a stile in trees. Beyond this is a signpost and map of the Mordiford Loop Walk. Turn right to reach a lane. Bear left on a bridleway and ignore a drive immediately to the right. After about 400 yards, take a right fork, following a track to reach a lane. Turn right, but after 20 yards go over a stile signed for the Wye Valley Walk. Cross two fields and go over a stile on to a lane. Turn left, then right at a bend, as waymarked, to go over two stiles. A further stile leads to a track into a forest. Leave the Mordiford Loop here to follow a track. Kink right, uphill, to reach a lovely dwelling and then go left through a gate. Drop down into a dip and take a track going right and uphill. This levels out and, after a considerable distance and ignoring all right turns, emerges on a lane by a pink cottage to the left. Turn right, then left by Forestry Commission sign for Haugh Wood. Go downhill, ignoring an arrow pointing right. Go past a right turn in a dip and, after 30 yards, note a path coming in from the left. About 25 yards beyond this, turn right and after a further 150 yards turn right again (as arrowed). Now go left into the trees and cross a plank over a stream. Go over a stile into a field. Cross this and two more fields, passing a farm, left, then go over a stile and follow a track to reach a lane by a pink cottage. Turn right, following the lane and ignoring all paths to reach a white cottage. Just beyond, go over a stile, left, into a field. Climb up to reach a stile into a wood. Continue up to a cottage, then go over a brow and straight down a tree lined path to reach a gate. Go through trees to reach a stile by a green gate. Go over and cross a field to reach another stile. Go over and bear left of a hill. Ahead is the spire of Fownhope Church: follow waymarkers through a housing estate and go left, passing a school to reach a road.

Head north-west along the B4224 to reach a lane, to the right, for Woolhope. Follow the road for a few hundred yards to reach a staircase to the left. Go up and take a path into woods. Take a right fork and climb steeply uphill through trees. Follow a thin ridge path through thick trees - this can be quite exciting - to reach a T-junction. Here, either go right to reach an open valley, crossing it to reach a house on the edge of conifers and a northward path to reach a lane for Mordiford, or go straight on along a forestry track. When this swings left, turn sharp right, almost doubling back, to reach a T-junction. Turn right to reach a stile. Go over and descend through an orchard to reach a gate. Go through and follow the B4224 back into Mordiford.

POINTS OF INTEREST:
Some of the best woodland in the county of Herefordshire.

REFRESHMENTS:
The Moon Inn, Mordiford.
The New Inn, Fownhope.
The Green Man, Fownhope.

Walk 94 LEINTWARDINE AND DOWNTON GORGE 9m (14$^1/_2$km)

Maps: OS Sheets Landranger 148; Pathfinder 951.

Open hills with beautiful views, woods and fields.

Start: At 404740, the large car parking area in Leintwardine.

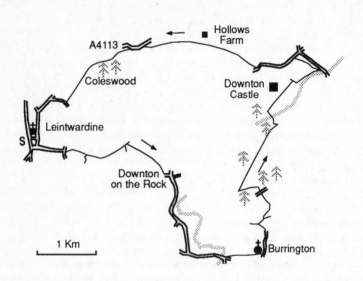

Head towards the River Teme, turning left just before the bridge and passing the Sun Inn to reach a T-junction. Go straight over to reach a signed path. Go steeply uphill under electricity cables to reach a farm track. Turn right to reach a disused, grassed over quarry. Further up, go through a gate to the left to reach a track. At the first right turn, go diagonally right through double gates and along an avenue of sycamore trees. Drop down and through a gate, and turn right through Downton on the Rock. Follow the lane through the village passing Bow Cottage, left, and descending through trees. At a T-junction, turn left to cross a humpback bridge over the River Teme. Immediately beyond, go left through a gate and stay close to a stream as you cross fields, with Burrington Church ahead. Go through a paddock and into the church grounds.

Exit the church grounds by some cottages and turn left. Go between farm buildings and continue on a signed concrete bridleway which climbs a hill and swings rightwards.

About 150 yards beyond the bend, go over a stile on the left and descend a field to cross a bridge over a stream. After a further 50 yards, go over a stile and up a field to find a gap in the far boundary. Go through and turn left along a track. Dip down, then cross towards trees to take a path through bracken. Go over a stile into a wood. Follow a path that rises to the left to reach a stile into a field. Go right towards a clump of trees to reach a gate, right, or a stile, further left, on to a vehicular track. Trend right through a gate and, after a few yards, go over a waymarked stile, left, and head diagonally right and downhill across a field to reach a fence. Follow the fence to reach a gate on to the track walked earlier. (The track can, of course, be followed directly to here). Go through a gate into the signed Downton Gorge Nature Reserve. Cross a bridge over the River Teme and take a track parallel to, but below, **Downton Castle**. Drop down to a cottage and go over a stile. Go left of the furthest cottage and through the first gate. Turn left and follow a riverside path. At a fine stone bridge, go left along a lane. Go left again to reach a cottage, to the right, and, beyond, go over a stile and cross a field. Bear left at the top to reach a stile and go over on to a lane. Turn left for $^1/_2$ mile passing a phone box and cottages. About 150 yards beyond these, turn right along a drive. Go through farm buildings and swing left to reach a large oak. Follow the fence right, then left, to reach a gate and go uphill to reach a stile in the top corner. Walk along a fence, then a hawthorn hedge, and bear right to reach a drive near a converted farm building. Follow the drive to a lane. Go right, then left to reach the A4113. Turn left, with care, but after a few yards turn left on a bridleway. Go through woods and into a field. Go left to a gate and right to a gap. Go left of a depression to reach another gate. Follow the track beyond to a lane and turn right. Follow the lane into Leintwardine, turning right alongside the church to reach the main road. Now turn left to return to the start.

POINTS OF INTEREST:
Downton Castle - The castle is actually a fortified mansion dating from 1778.

REFRESHMENTS:
Nothing on the walk, but ample choice in Leintwardine.

Walk 95   KING'S THORN AND HOARWITHY   9m (14½km)

Maps: OS Sheets Landranger 149; Pathfinder 1040.

Attractive paths more than compensate for the road sections.

Start: At 498322, the parking area on the minor road to King's Thorn.

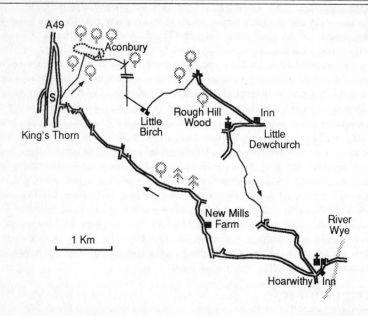

Walk north towards the main road and take the first drive on the right. Bend left by a rusty shack behind a hedge, then pass a house, on the left, with two sculptured horse heads on the gate. Where the drive goes off to the right, carry on through a kissing gate and, after 60 yards, take an uphill track where the main one veers left. Climb into mixed woodland, going over at cross-roads by a waymarker post. Turn right at a T-junction about 70 yards beyond. Go left to the trig. point on Aconbury Hill. The summit hillfort can be totally hidden by bracken and the hill-top is enclosed by trees, but it is a pleasant spot. From the trig point, bear right to regain the track by a more obvious earthwork slope. Follow the track to reach a stile by a gate and turn right, between hedgerows, to reach a lane by Priory Stone Cottage. Cross and take the lane beyond. Turn left at a cross-roads by a cottage with a walled garden, going along a green avenue to join a route coming in from the right. Follow this to reach two cottages (in Little Birch) on the right. Go through a gate opposite Greenlea Cottage and follow a green track, going through Merrivale Farm to reach a new gate. Go through and walk to another gate. Beyond, walk to a gate just left of the electricity cables. Go through and turn right along a lane. There are rights of way off this lane that lead directly to the church at Little Dewchurch, but they are difficult to find, so follow the lane into the village, turning right at a cross-roads to reach St David's Church, Little Dewchurch.

Follow the lane beyond the church and after about 400 yards look carefully to the left for Morriston, a farm across the small valley. There is a stile in a dip which may be overgrown: go over and descend to the valley to find a footpath sign on a post. Go right, following the line of electricity cables, cross a stream and follow the opposite bank. Go through a gate and turn right along a fence, then climb away left to reach an awkward stile on the right. Go over and take either a high route or a low route across two fields with the valley stream well down to the right. Follow a broad track diagonally right down to a long stone cottage. Follow the lane beyond, passing a distinctive black and white cottage, to a junction in Hoarwithy, with the New Harp Inn opposite. The village church, a local landmark with its relatively modern design and bell tower is to the left. Turn sharp right from the junction and follow a lane, bearing left once to reach the drive to New Mills Farm. Take the drive through the farm to reach a T-junction by a modern barn. Turn left along a track. Where the track forks by a gate, keep left along the woodland edge. Where this track splits at a hedge, take the right side, later rejoining the original track. Go past two houses either side and St Mary's Church, Little Birch to reach a T-junction. Go right, then left, following the lane across a cross-roads and back to King's Thorn and the start.

REFRESHMENTS:
The Plough Inn, Little Dewchurch.
The New Harp Inn, Hoarwithy.

Walk 96   WYRE FOREST (ROUTE 2)   9m (14½km)

Maps: OS Sheets Landranger 138; Pathfinder 932 and 952.
One of the best walks in the region.
Start: At 777763, the B4194 bridge over Dowles Brook.

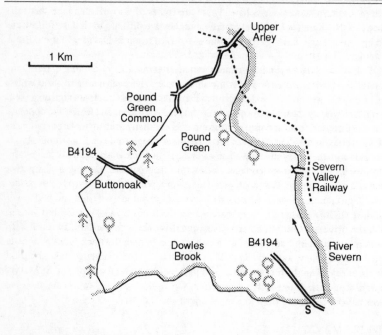

Go through a gate/stile on to a wide track that follows the Dowles Brook into the River Severn. Follow the Severn upstream and after passing a caravan park go under an aqueduct spanning the river (carrying Elan Valley water to Birmingham) to reach the wooded Arley Estate. Exit the wood by a cottage called 'Seckley'. Go over a stile into more open land. Go under the **Victoria Bridge** and cross fields, the last is a picnic site in summer, then turn right over a footbridge into Arley village. Go up past the Harbour Inn to Arley Station. Follow the lane to the New Inn. Opposite the inn is Arbour Farm. Go through this on a track leading to Pound Green Common. At the first cottage, leave the track for a green path on to the common. Go past a refurbished cottage, left, then turn right by a bungalow behind cropped firs. Leave this wide track almost immediately for a green track which bears right to pass a large house on the left. Cross a wide track and go over a stile into tall conifers. Now either go right at a yellow waymarker arrow to reach a stile into the garden of a cottage, exiting over another stile on to a road (B4149), or ignore the arrow and go straight on through wooden buildings to reach the road lower down. Cross the B4194 by Clematis Cottage to reach a forest car park. Go up a wide ride to meet another coming in from the right. Cross a wide green ride, following the forestry track for $^3/_4$ mile to reach an artificial pond.

Go left on a track with a sign 'Warning, maximum load 3 tonnes gross'. Cross a bridge over the Dowles brook. The next section of the walk is excellent for butterfly spotters. Go past a post with blue and yellow arrows and bear left after 100 yards to cross a stream feeding the Dowles Brook. Go up and contour along to a bridge over the Brook. Turn right at the T-junction, passing Cooper's Mill, an outward bound centre. About 200 yards beyond, bear right, keeping the lower track. Cross a stream and pass Knowles Mill (National Trust). Pass a white house, right, a stone cottage, left, then go over a bridge. On a bend where cars are often parked, enter the signed Fred Dale Nature Reserve. Go right, up steps, then turn left along an old railway to reach the B4194 at the start of the walk.

POINTS OF INTEREST:
Victoria Bridge – Built in 1851 and still carrying steam trains, now on the Severn Valley Railway, a private line.

REFRESHMENTS:
The Harbour Inn, Arley.
The New Inn, on the route.

Walk 97   EWYAS HAROLD AND ABBEY DORE   9m (14$\frac{1}{2}$km)

Maps: OS Sheets Landranger 149; Pathfinder 1063 and 1039.

Some climbing to link two contrasting waterways, the Dulas and Dore rivers.

Start: At 388287, in Ewyas Harold.

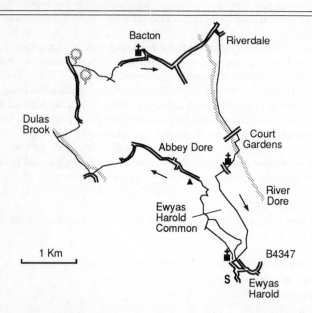

Walk round the churchyard and go past the new bungalows beyond to reach a stile into a field. Go to the top left corner and take a track, left, which skirts the common. Go past the front of the 'Weaver's Place' and through the garden to 'Prince's Place'. Turn left at a gate on to a wide path, following it to a cottage. Go left and soon go through a gate on to the common. Scattered stone houses cover the common which is typical heathland, with good views of the Black Mountains. Go rightwards to reach a good track by a wind pump. Follow the track (not shown on the OS Landranger) going through a series of kinks to reach the trig point. Continue to reach a lane and turn left towards Newton. Turn left just beyond Hollingwood Farm, to the right, and descend a steep, narrow lane to cross a bridge over the Dulas Brook. Go up to a road and turn right. Go just past a garage and turn right through a gate to follow the Dulas

Brook. Stay with the brook, in fine surroundings, for about $\frac{1}{2}$ mile, then cross a footbridge to the right. Climb up a field, with Upper Cefn Farm right, to meet a sunken track coming from the farm. Go through the gate opposite and trend leftwards across a field. Go over a low fence on to a lane and turn left.

Follow the lane to the end of a wood and turn right through a gate to go along the edge of the wood to reach an unfenced piece of woodland. Walk through this to reach a gate, to the right, into a field. Go across the middle of the field, through two more gates and along the left hedge. Go through a further two gates on to a farm track. Go through the second of two gates on the left and follow a track to a gate at the far right corner of a field. Do not go through: instead, go left along a hedge, with a cottage and pond to the right. Go left on a wide track which bends right to reach a lane by **St Faith's Church, Bacton**. Turn right, downhill, to a T-junction with the B4347. Walk ahead to cross the River Dore and then turn right to pass 'Riverdale' going through a gate into a field and taking a farm track which bears right to reach a stile. Go over and follow a waymarked path, with stiles, which hugs the river and eventually reaches a lane. Turn left and then first right through Abbey Dore Court. Go right on a signed path. Turn left through a kissing gate and go left along the river. Cross by footbridge and cross two fields to reach **Abbey Dore**. Opposite the abbey there is a path veering slightly right up a field: take this, going over a fence and walking uphill to reach another fence. Turn left along it to reach a gate on to the Common. From here there is a choice of paths back to **Ewyas Harold**.

POINTS OF INTEREST:

St Faith's Church, Bacton – The church featured in the film *On the Black Hill*.

Abbey Dore - This Cistercian monastery was built in the 12th century. It had control over 17 local farms and its wool commanded a high price. Abandoned after the Dissolution, it was restored and converted into the parish church by Lord Scudamore and the architect/craftsman John Abel in 1633.

Ewyas Harold - The village's first name derives from either a place of sheep or a place of yew trees. Harold derives from a legend that King Harold survived the Battle of Hastings, despite the eye wound, and was brought here to recover. The story tells that the King became a hermit.

REFRESHMENTS:

The Neville Arms, Abbey Dore.

There is a café (seasonal openings) at Abbey Dore Court and several opportunities in Ewyas Harold.

Walks 98 & 99   HAY BLUFF AND BLACK HILL   9½m (15km)
or 10½m (17km)

Maps: OS Sheets Landranger 161; Pathfinder 1039 and 1016.

The most spectacular walk in Herefordshire, with several miles above 2000 feet.

Start: At 239373, at a fork of minor roads.

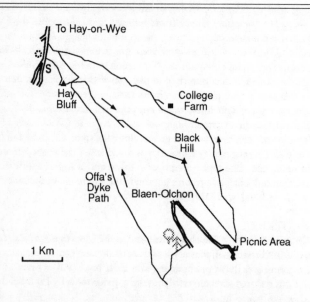

Please note that this is a proper mountain walk requiring all necessary gear and rations. Try to choose a good weather spell, as the route is very exposed to the elements.

From the upland common, close to a stone circle marked on the OS map, climb towards Hay Bluff, either ascending direct or using one of the obvious switchback tracks to the top. The summit is in a superb position, offering great views over much of southern Wales. The scarp slope to Twmpa holds the gaze and Pen y Gader Fawr and Waun Fach are notable across the moor. A discernible path from the summit trig point heads for a wide domed hill. At its base, the path divides: keep left, contouring on a thin path overlooking the upper Monnow Valley. Crib y Garth, or Black Hill, is the distant promontory ahead. The way stays close to the scarp edge then ascends steadily to the summit with views to the Olchon Valley to the right. Beyond the summit trig point the ridge becomes narrow but the rocky obstacles can mostly be avoided. Walk the 'Cat's Back', as this ridge is called, and begin to descend carefully and with maintained interest to reach a picnic spot at the end of a minor road.

The shorter, lower, route goes left along the base of the Cat's Back on a track lined with hawthorns. After about a mile, a gate leads to a metalled bridleway underneath trees. Ignore all right turns, staying with the bridleway to cross a stream and kink right, then left. Go through a gate and walk along field edges with a slope dropping away rightwards, linking the fields by gates. Pass a huge stone tablet by a hawthorn, eventually leaving the valley to climb steadily on to Hay Common. The best line now is a central one, crossing the common then veering round the base of Hay Bluff to suddenly reach the mountain road and start point.

The longer route from the picnic spot goes down the winding lane and turns right at a junction. Stay with the lane as it loops around to cross the Olchon Brook. About $^3/_4$ mile past this distinct bend take a path attacking the hillside to the right. A good guide is an enclosure of trees some yards to the right on the mountain side. Go through a small rock band - this offers no problem - and bear leftwards to join the **Offa's Dyke Path**. Turn right along the Path. Go past some painted boulders and climb up the easily graded broad ridge of Llech y Lladron. Now descend peaty slopes to meet the path from Hay Bluff used on the outward route. Retrace your steps back to the start.

POINTS OF INTEREST:
Offa's Dyke Path - This fine National Trail runs from Chepstow to Prestatyn. The section on the Black Mountains is the most exposed, the Path choosing a mainly downland route through the Welsh borders. The Dyke itself was constructed by the Saxon King Offa for reasons that are still not fully understood. It was most probably defensive, keeping incursions by the Welsh to a minimum, but may also have been a method of controlling and taxing trade between the Welsh and the Saxons.

REFRESHMENTS:
None on the route, but there are excellent options in Hay on Wye.

Walk 100 WEOBLEY, DILWYN AND KINGS PYON 10m (16km)

Maps: OS sheets Landranger 149; Pathfinder 994.
Classic black and white villages set in quiet countryside.
Start: At 402517, in Weobley village.

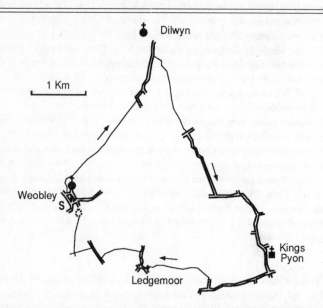

Take one of two parallel streets to reach the church. Either route makes a turn right to reach four gates. There is a stile by the second gate to the left. Go over and walk along a hedge, crossing several fields on a thin path to reach a cattle shed/stone barn. Now bear left from the main track to reach a gate into a field. Go towards a corner of a wood to reach a gate. At the end of the wood, keep straight ahead to reach a gate with a footpath sign. The village of Dilwyn can now be seen: follow the obvious lane towards it, noting a stile on the right just beyond two modern houses. Dilwyn has a village green and some excellent timber-framed houses. Retrace your steps to the noted stile, now on the left. Go over it and another and, after about 200 yards, cross a footbridge and bear right by the power cables. Go over a stile, noting a clump of trees about 150 yards to the right, the site of an old moat. Cross a footbridge over a stream and bear slightly right away from the hedge to reach a stile in a hedge. Go over and take a central line across a field, with an orchard 50 yards to the left. Bear left under the power cables and go through a gate. Cross a lane and go down the lane opposite to reach, eventually, a T-junction. Turn left to a junction and there turn right on a lane signed for Kings Pyon and Canon Pyon. From this lane there is a distant view, to the left, of the Clee Hills, while ahead, over the farm buildings, is the tree-crested Pyon Hill. Pass 'The Hill', set back on the left. Go through Kings Pyon village to reach a cross-roads. Turn right and go along the lane to reach Wistaston, a large farm to the right. Turn along its drive, passing between the house and the outbuildings and turning left at the end of the large cattle shed to reach a waymarker post and gate. Go diagonally right across a field to reach a waymarked stile in the left-hand corner. Go over and follow the left hedge. Just before a very broad oak tree, kink into the next field and, after 150 yards, reach a concealed pair of stiles over a ditch just right of a copse. Go straight across the field ahead, cross an awkward stile and head for a gate just left of a red cottage. Go through and turn left along a lane. Turn first right and first right again and walk to a spreading oak. Go through a gate, left, under this tree and aim for the large farm ahead. Go over a stile on the right and walk towards the farm, going around a drystone wall and along the farm drive to reach a lane. Turn right. After 200 yards there is a lodge: just beyond, take a track on the left. Go through two gates, following power cables, and where there is a gate, to the left, with a footpath sign, go right on a twin track which swings away towards Weobley church spire. Go over a stile and through a gate. Cross a field to reach another stile and gate by large oaks. Now pass the ancient 'ring and bailey' to reach **Weobley**.

POINTS OF INTEREST:

Weobley - The village church is 13th/14th century and has the second highest spire in Herefordshire. Elsewhere in the village there are many beautiful black and white buildings, good examples being the Red Lion, the Unicorn Inn, the Mansion House, and the Salutation Inn.

REFRESHMENTS:

The Crown Inn, Dilwyn.
Any of the beautiful inns in Weobley, as mentioned above.